#1 INTERNATIONAL BEST SELLER

# Voices of INFLUENCE

## THE UNTOLD STORIES OF REMARKABLE SPEAKERS

ZAHRINA ROBERTSON
SHARLENE LICCIARDELLO
JACKIE BREASLEY
JO WORTHY
RACHEL PLEASANT
ANGELA SEDRAN

KAMA ATCHESON
PINKY MCKAY
RACHEL ANASTASI
SALLY PROWSE
PRIYA RAVINDRA KALYANIMATH
HEIDI STENSCHKE

www.evolveglobalpublishing.com

© Copyright 2023
By **Zahrina Robertson**
and Sharlene Licciardello, Jackie Breasley, Jo Worthy, Rachel Pleasant, Angela Sedran, Kama Atcheson, Pinky McKay, Rachel Anastasi, Sally Prowse, Priya Ravindra Kalyanimath, Heidi Stenschke

Edited by James North
All rights reserved.

Book Layout ©2023
Published by:
Evolve Global Publishing
www.EvolveGlobalPublishing.com

No part of this book may be reproduced or transmitted in any form or by any means, electronic or mechanical, including photocopying, recording or by any information storage and retrieval system, without written permission from the authors, except for the inclusion of brief quotations in a review.

**Limit of Liability Disclaimer:** The information contained in this book is for information purposes only, and may not apply to your situation. The author, publisher, distributor, and provider provide no warranty about the content or accuracy of the content enclosed. The information provided is subjective. Keep this in mind when reviewing this guide. Neither the Publisher nor the Author shall be liable for any loss of profit or any other commercial damages resulting from the use of this guide. All links are for information purposes only and are not warranted for content, accuracy, or any other implied or explicit purpose.

**Earnings Disclaimer:** All income examples in this book are examples. They are not intended to represent or guarantee that everyone will achieve the same results. You understand that each individual's success will be determined by his or her desire, dedication, background, effort, and motivation to work. There is no guarantee you will duplicate any of the results stated here. You recognize any business endeavours have inherent risk or loss of capital.

**Voices of Influence: The Untold Stories of Remarkable Speakers**
1st Edition. 2023
Interior V4
Fonts: Minion Pro
Page size: 6" x 9"

ASIN: B0CNL94XWV (Amazon Kindle)
ISBN: 978-0-6454380-9-3 (eBook)
ISBN: 978-0-6486231-0-6 (Amazon Paperback)
ISBN: 978-0-6486231-2-0 (Amazon Hardcover)
ISBN: 978-0-6486231-3-7 (Ingram Spark) PAPERBACK
ISBN: 978-0-6486231-1-3 (Ingram Spark) HARDCOVER
ISBN: 978-0-6454380-9-3 (Smashwords)

**CONTACT THE AUTHOR:**
Author Website: www.zahrina.com
Contact: Zahrina Robertson
Email: zahrina@zahrina.com

**TRADEMARKS**

All product names, logos, and brands are the property of their respective owners. All company, product, and service names used in this book are for identification purposes only. Using these names, logos, and brands does not imply endorsement. All other trademarks cited herein are the property of their respective owners.

# Table of Contents

Introduction ........................................................................................... 7
The Authors .......................................................................................... 9
Chapter 1 - The Art of Radical Reinvention by *Zahrina Robertson* ...... 13
Chapter 2 - The Power of Rewriting Your
               Life Story by *Sharlene Licciardello* ...................................... 27
Chapter 3 - Madame Butterfly – Living with
               Disability by Jackie Breasley ................................................. 41
Chapter 4 - Rise, Woman, Rise - Finding Your
               "Eye of The Tiger" by *Jo Worthy* ........................................ 53
Chapter 5 - Shattering Glass Ceilings: One woman's commitment
               to empowering women to take their seats at
               the corporate table by *Rachel Pleasant* ............................... 67
Chapter 6 - Brighter than the Sun: A Journey from
               Trials to Triumph in Leadership by *Angela Sedran* ......... 81
Chapter 7 - Your Health is your Wealth by *Kama Atcheson* ............... 95
Chapter 8 - Proud to be Loud by *Pinky McKay* ................................. 109
Chapter 9 - Becoming Free To Be Me by *Rachel Anastasi* ................. 123
Chapter 10 - A Man is Not a Financial Plan by *Sally Prowse* ............. 137
Chapter 11 - Your Life, Your Purpose,
                Your Pace by *Priya Ravindra Kalyanimath* ..................... 149
Chapter 12 - The F -Word. And It's Not What
                You Think; It's How by *Heidi Stenschke* ........................ 161

• • • •

# Introduction

*By Zahrina Robertson*

Dreams do come true... for a while, I had a dream to produce a very special collaboration of untold stories by fellow like-minded, heartfelt females with great values. This collaboration has been the highlight of my career. I truly believe you will find yourself deeply immersed within the thought-provoking and mesmerizing stories of "Voices of Influence: The Untold Stories of Remarkable Speakers."

Get ready to embark on a transformative journey as twelve extraordinary female authors bare their souls, sharing tales of courage, resilience, and the profound art of reinvention. This anthology is not merely a collection of stories; it is a tapestry of empowerment woven by dynamic keynote speakers who have transcended the boundaries of convention to shape narratives that resonate with the core of the human experience.

As you delve into the heart of this remarkable collection, prepare to be captivated by the untold stories that have shaped the lives of these extraordinary women.

Each author is a maestro of the spoken word, a virtuoso on the stage, and now, a storyteller on these pages. Their words, like a symphony of courage, will reverberate through your being, leaving an indelible mark on your soul to take action.

In a world inundated with noise, "Voices of Influence" shines as a beacon of authenticity, offering an oasis of genuine human connection. The authors have courageously peeled back the layers of their lives, revealing the trials and triumphs that have sculpted them into the influential speakers they are today.

This is not just a book; it is an invitation to witness the metamorphosis of strength, vulnerability, and the unyielding spirit that resides within every woman.

The journey through these stories is akin to a rollercoaster of emotions, each turn of the page unlocking a new facet of resilience and empowerment. From navigating personal setbacks to conquering professional challenges, the narratives within "Voices of Influence" are a testament to the power of reinvention, something I hold close to my heart.

These women have not only embraced change; they have become architects of transformation, shaping their destinies with unwavering determination.

*"Voices of Influence"* is not just an anthology; it is a catalyst for personal and collective transformation. The narratives within these pages will seep into your consciousness, sparking a metamorphosis that transcends the realms of storytelling.

This is an invitation to embrace the power of reinvention, to find inspiration in the shared experiences of these dynamic speakers, and to embark on a journey of self-discovery that will leave an enduring impact on your life.

**Get ready to be re-ignited, re-set, and re-invented!**

This special journey awaits you, and I hope the voices within these pages influence your heart, not just your reading experience, but the very fabric of your existence. Welcome to a literary odyssey where every word is a stepping stone toward a more empowered and enlightened you.

Happy reading!

**Zahrina Robertson**
*Global Multi-Award Winning Brand Visionary Expert, Keynote Speaker, Photographer, Videographer, Author, and Artist*

# The Authors

**Zahrina Robertson**
*Global Keynote Speaker, Accomplished Author of 5 books, Global Multi-Award Winning Brand Visionary Expert, Photographer, Videographer, Author, and Artist*

🌐 Zahrina.com / ZahrinaPhotography.com / ZahrinaGallery.com

in Zahrina Robertson

f ZahrinaPhotographyandVideo / ZahrinaGallery

@Zahrina_Photography_Video @ZahrinaGallery

**Sharlene Licciardello**
*Visionary Author, Life Coach, and Co-Founder of "Rewrite Your Life Story"*

 rewriteyourlifestory.com.au

**Jackie Breasley**
*Global Keynote Speaker, Disability Thought Leader and Author*

in linkedin.com/in/jackie-breasley-71736876

🌐 jackiebreasley.consulting

### Jo Worthy
*Global Keynote Speaker, Founder of the Worthy Women Movement, and Author*

 worthywomenmovement.com

 facebook.com/groups/worthywomanmovement

### Rachel Pleasant
*Global Keynote Speaker and Founder of 'Your Seat at the Table', Marketing Leader*

 yourseatatthetable.com

 linkedin.com/company/your-seat-at-the-table-official

### Angela Sedran
*Global Keynote Speaker, Strategy and Leadership Consultant, Coach and Mentor*

 angelasedran.com

 linkedin.com/in/angelasedran

 @yourbadassbusinesscoach / @theladybossbusinesscoach

### Kama Atcheson
*Global Keynote Speaker, Elite Woman in Finance (MPA Magazine, 2022)*

 linkedin.com/in/kama-atcheson-1b51279

**Pinky McKay**
*Global Keynote TEDx Speaker, International Board-Certified Lactation Consultant (IBCLC), Best-selling Author, Podcast Host*

🌐 *pinkymckay.com / boobiefoods.com.au*

in *linkedin.com/in/pinky-mckay-04910a203*

f *facebook.com/pinky.mckay.fanpage*

📷 *@pinkymckayofficial*

B *pinkymckay.com/blog*

**Rachel Anastasi**
*Global Keynote Speaker, Coach, Author, NLP practitioner, Psychosomatic Therapist & Teacher, Medium/intuitive*

f *Rachel Amy Anastasi*

*rachel@rachelanastasi.com*

**Sally Prowse**
*Global Keynote Speaker, Founder and CEO Sandcastle Finance*

🌐 *sandcastlefinance.com.au*

in *linkedin,com/in/sallyprowse*

f *facebook.com/sandcastlefinance*

📷 *@sandcastlefinance*

**Priya Ravindra Kalyanimath**
*Global Keynote Speaker, Founder and CEO, Punar, Company Director -GAICD*

 *punar.com.au*

 *au.linkedin.com/company/punar*

 *instagram.com/punar.co*

 *facebook.com/Punar.co*

**Heidi Stenschke**
*Global Keynote Speaker, Coach, EMDR Clinician, Hypnotherapist, Yoga Teacher, Master Practitioner and Trainer of Neuro-Linguistic Programming (NLP), Founder of Hypnoga®*

 *heidiannietta.com*

Chapter 1

# The Art of Radical Reinvention

**Zahrina Robertson**
*Global Keynote Speaker, Accomplished Author of 5 books, Global Multi-Award Winning Brand Visionary Expert, Photographer, Videographer, Author, and Artist*

## About The Author: Zahrina Robertson

With a stellar reputation spanning 15 years as a multi-award-winning global authority, Zahrina Robertson stands at the forefront of Personal Branding. Zahrina's career spans working at LVMH in marketing and branding, working on managing brands like global brands like Dior, Kenzo, Marc Jacobs, and Guerlain, regularly executing million-dollar launches with top fashion labels.

Her personal brand visual expertise includes working with Sir Richard Branson, Arnold Schwarzenegger, Simon Sinek, Tim Ferris, and Aviva Drescher to name a few. Zahrina crafts narratives that transcend the ordinary, reshaping the way individuals perceive and present their personal brand. Zahrina is a key person of influence, whom people love to collaborate with.

As an accomplished author of five business books, plus a children's book, Zahrina's words communicate transformative wisdom, guiding readers on a journey of self-discovery and reinvention. Her insights, meticulously woven into the fabric of her writings, empower individuals to embrace change as a catalyst for growth.

Zahrina's talents extend beyond the written word. Her natural spark commands stages globally as a dynamic motivational keynote speaker and artist. Armed with charisma and a deep understanding of the intricacies of personal branding, she captivates audiences, leaving an indelible mark on the collective psyche. Zahrina has a waitlist of mentoring entrepreneurs for true success.

In a world where personal brand and the art of visual storytelling has become a crucial currency, Zahrina Robertson illuminates the path for others to navigate the complex landscape of self-presentation. In a disruptive world, book Zahrina to speak at your next conference. Her commitment to changing the world through the power of her radical reinvention formula makes her a beacon of inspiration for those ready to embark on their transformative journey.

• • • •

**L***ights! Camera! Action!*

I clearly remember that surreal moment, being interviewed on national TV, not by one but three uber-keen journalists about my story. I was being broadcasted out to millions of people's TVs and phones... and suddenly I felt a deep sense of calm and a strong desire washed over me, then a message speared into my heart:

> **"Zahrina, you now need to help as many people as possible."**

Let me take you on a rollercoaster ride of self-reflection, from thinking I knew who I was and where I wanted to go, to feeling lost in despair. Through the fog, I was finally able to see the signposts to radically reinventing myself! I hope my journey will inspire you to not give up, ride out the anxiety of any fear-based scenarios, and really get to the other side where everything starts to make sense. Here we go…

Have you ever felt it's your time to shine… but then you don't? Your time to take charge, but then you didn't listen to your gut. This was me – unfortunately, I listened to my ego and felt my heart sink to the bottom of the ocean like the Titanic.

**Warning signs were EVERYWHERE.**

My established business and brand identity had been stolen and I was being stalked by a competitor, hell-bent on ruining my reputation and stealing my ideas. Layer upon layer piled on me until I was stuck in the sheets of that sloppy lasagna of lies. Have you ever felt other people want to dim your light? Overwhelmed, I didn't know how to get out... was this the tipping point?

No, my spiritual awakening was my tipping point.

Being named "The Annie Leibovitz of Branding" and "Photographer to the Stars," I showed up as a multi-award-winning, high-energy achiever. I feel things instinctively – in my gut and through my lens of creativity. Despite all this, I found myself isolated and not solving the problem I was experiencing of identity theft. Even though my head was pounding, my heart was hurting. Gradually, I gave into procrastination and fear.

Basically, I stopped being me. Can you relate to a time you were stuck in no-man's-land? No matter how deep the layers of that lasagna piled up, nothing was moving me into action.

I didn't consider myself a victim. In fact, I've lived my life as a victor.

Well, that's what I thought.

Being a first-generation Australian, alongside my brother, I had a high sense of awareness of how fortunate we were to be born in "the lucky country," Australia. Mum and Dad immigrated from England to start their dream life. Despite inheriting creative genes from my dad (not his Omar Sharif looks!) and my sheer determination from my mum, I had lost my creative mojo.

I pushed myself to climb to the top of the mountain, and lo and behold, I got my T-shirt! The mountain climbing, however, sucked the energy out of me. Upon deep reflection, I realised I wasn't living a conscious life. I was isolated in loss and silence. The daily activities I once enjoyed now felt like moving concrete blocks up the tallest mountain in the universe.

**Humans are naturally creative.**

When we lose this creative mojo, it calls for a renewal or reinvention of self. Having worked with Richard Branson, Arnold Schwarzenegger, Simon Sinek, Aviva Dresher, Matt Church, and Carla Zampatti, as well as collaborating with thought leaders, coaches, speakers, and authors, I'm known as the Queen of Personal Branding, yet I'd lost my mojo! I'm so grateful to experience first-hand the privilege of being the main conduit of reinventing thousands of smart people throughout my career. However, my own looming reinvention was about to light up the stratosphere on a starry night! And I didn't see this blazing comet coming.

So how did I end up in this dark place?

For a good solid five years, I lived in ego and stopped tuning into my intuition. Along the way, I'd lost my self-belief and confidence in my decisions… I shrugged off bad experiences as just the hard knocks of life, not realizing these were clear signals to a better me and a better life. Damn, hindsight is great, isn't it?

Have you ever felt like a leaf, floating doomed towards a massive waterfall? That was me! I allowed my power to flow away to the egomaniacs in my world who were disorientating my soul. I was a "yes" girl to the wrong people, leading to confusion and a lack of focus. After 10 years of building brilliant, dynamic personal brands for others to succeed, I've come to the realisation that some people are takers, and others are givers. Don't give your power away.

**Your soul deserves more than you know. Watch out for the signals.**

One day, I worked with Michelle Hamdorf, one of the most intriguing clients my camera has ever laid eyes on. Her energy was right off the Richter scale! Michelle was a force. Her incredible energy and life force were so strong I felt her in my soul. We were dancing in my sunny studio, which is filled with natural light. We were having so much fun, laughing, and enjoying each other's company. I was taking the most incredible branding images of Michelle. She brought four suitcases filled with designer clothes, jewellery, shoes, and bags. We were dancing the rhumba in the light.

Suddenly, Michelle said, "STOP! Zahrina, I have to tell you something very important."

"OK, I'm all ears," I nodded, full of curiosity.

Pointing to the front of her forehead, Michelle said with intensity and calmness, "I have a tumour."

I was floored! I nearly fainted and felt completely numb. I felt like I was having an out-of-body experience, in slow motion. I was empty in just that instant. I had no words. I had two cameras on each hip, weighing around eight kilos and I nearly dropped the camera in my hands.

With the light glowing behind her, Michelle then said the most profound statement of my career.

"I've done all my research and there's no one in Australia who could curate my message to produce the world's best images, and truly showcase my soul to allow me to live my legacy fully. This is the reason I'm here with you Zahrina; you truly are the "Queen of Brand Photography and Video" and no one comes close to your talent, believe me, angel."

I gulped and stammered, "Oooh, thank you so very much, I'm in total shock, and I'm truly grateful, Michelle... tell me, what's your legacy, my darling?"

"I'm here to get on as many boards as possible to help the next generation of women know that it is possible to achieve their dreams. The only way to do this is to be noticed and seen in the right way, the authentic way, and with energy in my eyes so that I connect to the heart of those I'm helping." Michelle said. Michelle Hamdorf did exactly this and served on numerous boards after our epic branding shoot before she passed away five months later.

I felt in my heart that Michelle was my signal, opportunity, and choice to be the best version I can be for the rest of my life; to live my life filled with creativity and passion on my terms, and to help others fulfill their dreams.

**This is why radical reinvention is an art form.**

Why have I gone through this to rise like a phoenix—like I know you can. I'm here to lead as many men and women to radical reinvention as possible. Michelle launched me on this mission.

I soon realized that heart-centered humans are my go-to humans. They have turned into my best clients, and often become my dearest friends. We click with others who have similar value systems and hold space for us and our hearts. Life is not a one-sided track. It's a long game.

Finding your tribe is key to loving your brand's direction. When I regained my creative mojo, my outlook and perspective dramatically changed from dark to light. The murky waters cleared to the divine Tiffany blue colour found in tropical island seas.

"Ooh no, I'm not an artist, I just pick up a camera." Over the course of my career, and in interviews, I had been reluctant to call myself an "artist". Yet, intuition directs me to press the button on my camera once, not a million times. Innately, I pick up the energy and emotions of humans with astounding accuracy, leading me to style many clients over the years.

Knowing what exceptional style looks like on a person is fun. What I do see is the inner light of the person; this is my superpower. Fun fact, I've never used professional lighting to photograph a client. For over 15 years, I've simply used natural light to capture the essence of them at their best; I just hold the camera.

"Yikes! I am an artist!" I declared in a recent podcast interview. One morning, I had a positive, physical reaction to coloured paint in an art video while scrolling on my phone. Out of the blue, I painted a few canvases, let myself loose, and

started enjoying the freedom of something brand new. My instincts whispered, "Have a different kind of today, Zahrina. A day where your heart connects to the art." This letting go released me into freedom after being held back; I found I was experiencing peace within. Art suddenly fuelled my fire. It opened me up to opportunities and making choices that drive me daily.
I talk about looking out for important signals.

Signals I've had include manifesting my own radical reinvention and feeling led to host my own retreats to guide many others. It's been a game-changer. Join me!

The hardest part about losing my creative mojo was feeling a loss of grace. In the past, I would 'live in grit,' following formulas, and other people's methods and now I choose to live in grace over grit. Grace is a superior way of living and being. Living in grit, I felt embarrassed, naked, and sensed the judgment of others. Living in grace is being in flow and freedom is my mantra. When living in grit, the pain was hard to bear, especially on my own. I looked inward and created a daily practice of meditation, that led me down a magnificent path of self-love and self-healing.

**Beauty is a lens provided by love.**

I fully comprehend how dark and deep that pit can be. Not only creative, sensitive people go through this pain of emptiness, that 'dark night of the soul.' Why do it alone? Tune in to your awareness, to a bigger 'why.'

It's like grieving; you have to wait for time to heal. Not quitting, but rather reinventing yourself to explore other avenues in the short time you have here. So, don't give up on your main game. Instead, get above the grit and move on. The phoenix is on the rise.

Intuition has led me to facilitate the greatest opportunities to host workshops and keynote speaking events globally.

Just imagine how you would feel, living heart-centered.

Perhaps you are yearning to reinvent yourself, however, fear holds you back. With the reliance on social media and fear-based news, many people are not tuning in; they are tuning out. Most of all, they are not tuning in to their heart. They are not on the right frequency, missing the signals, opportunities, and choices for their success. If this is you, your authentic self is yet to be discovered.

When we stop and go within, this is all we need. Wouldn't you love to come back to authenticity, to radically reinvent your brand and yourself from the inside out? It's often said that life doesn't give us what we want; it gives us what we need. So you're only ever on the path to your purpose, no matter where that path wanders.

That said, old behaviours must go and we need to be ready to rise up. We also must be in tune with our emotions. Whatever feelings you suppress through distractions or overeating or channelling into something, they will not go away. They may even get bigger.

We might also suppress ourselves when we're young and forming our personality. Speaking is my superpower. In an explosion of activity, I now talk on stage, paint on stage, and help people to see life differently – so different from the shy young girl I used to be.

Recently I painted onstage and raised enough money to send three female victims of domestic violence on a retreat to receive self-love. All we have is love, and for this, we don't need anything else. Radically reinventing myself has left me more radiant, reawakened, and revitalised. It is an art form, that's why I do what I do.

Radical reinvention is about being truly clear about what we want in our new chapter – after all, we are not here on Earth for that long. I've climbed the mountain, got the T-shirt, and now it's time to climb another mountain: Mount Reinvention.

**Your personal brand is your name.**

One day a fellow businesswoman said my first book, 'Magnetic Branding ' all my images needed to include business names alongside the person's images I had taken.

WOW! I'm super happy, I stuck to my guns of not including business names because my book would have dated immediately after people resigned from businesses or sold their businesses.

Your name is your trademark, our most treasured real estate. It's our brand.

My point is that my dad named me Zahrina a unique name. We are not a logo, we're all unique, and we reinvent and evolve.

He wanted me to be different, to stand out....however, he stood out and taught me a lot early on about radical reinvention.

Dad's life journey was an inspiration to me. He migrated from India to Birmingham. He arrived in Australia when he met Mum. Mum was a nurse and Dad loved what her medical textbooks were teaching about the body. He then trained and became a nurse, much to the surprise of the family. He progressed to become a psychiatric nurse. Throughout his life, he was a photographer, too.

Necessity being the mother of invention, when Mum and Dad could not get a job due to prejudice in Queensland in the late 1980s, they resourcefully opened up an Indian restaurant. At a young age, I was privy to my own parent's personal reinvention. Closing the restaurant after six years, we moved back to Sydney.

Dad then retired and, after taking up woodworking as a hobby, he became an inventor. He won an international gold medal award in Geneva, Switzerland for his groundbreaking AngleMag tool for woodworking. The story of his clever invention was written about in national magazines. He even had two streets in Canberra, Australia named after him; AngleMag Street and Jeff Snell Street.

Looking into my past, reinvention has always been in my genes. It takes courage to harness this for the good of humanity. Now I'm fully grateful for the series of events that led to my dark night of the soul because without it I might still be wandering, ego-driven, and worrying about what others think.

There comes a realisation in life, that what you do with your life matters. No one can take this away from you, except yourself. I was uncertain too… until I took the step of taking photos of my art for my social profiles and Instagram under @zahrinaartist. Those photos enabled a miraculous opportunity to fly to New York where I exhibited my new works in a fine art gallery – definitely a pinch-me moment! WOW, me? Was this happening?

A couple of years earlier, I was invited to New York to speak to top businesswomen on all things relating to personal branding and reinvention… all of this is not a coincidence. It's a signal.

**Art is hope. Hope is everything.**

Few people believe they can create a new career from something they are passionate about or have just discovered. Little did I know 20 years ago that I could write five books, including a children's book, and become an accidental artist, a mum, keynote speaker working with others to build their global personal brand.

If I hadn't taken that first leap of faith to just start painting and listening to my heart… none of that would ever have happened. If you feel you're in the swamp now, there is a path forward. Allow me to share three parts of my unique formula, The Art of Radical Reinvention to help you progress:

### The Signal

Ask yourself, "Am I tired of this?"

Recently, a fellow school mum, Sally, and I were chatting about her life. Sally shared how her life was spinning past her so fast. She expressed how much her life was missing meaning and how much she hated her corporate job.

Sally shared with me her "dream job" in the greatest of detail. I asked her how long she had been thinking about changing careers and she sadly said, "Ten years."

I was floored. "Ten years is too long, girlfriend! Let's develop a strategy to create a new pathway to success!"

She booked in a day session with me to help build her radical reinvention strategy. Now Sally is shimmying along her new path to freedom and enjoying her dream job. She has a reinvigorated, positive outlook on her life and family. Finally, her life is much more balanced and she is 100% fulfilled.

Success stories fuel my global movement to create change in the hearts of my community of Radical Reinventors. Are you joining us?

Never be scared to listen to yourself. Our gut controls intuition and helps with decisions, while our heart controls feelings, and yes, it hurts sometimes! Our mind keeps balance and logic in our choices.

Deeply listening to my intuition led my heart to make easy decisions when standing at the fork in the road. Keep open to your signals.

### The Opportunity

How you show up in the little moments is where your opportunities will show up.

Have you ever had a regret? A business decision you didn't make that turned out to be a great opportunity? Were you listening to someone else? Or yourself? Taking our eyes off what we already know, and not connecting to our internal story will all lead to missed opportunities. The day I started painting I got past my self-doubt and just picked up the brush. Self-sabotage can steal your opportunities.

When you make values-based decisions, you will start to attract not only good people but a values-based tribe. I continue to grow my community with brilliant, grounded women and men in business. Interesting opportunities will always appear; write them down. Relate your purpose to these opportunities. By having faith, your next step will take you where you need to be. Trust the process.

### The Choice

Ditch the perfectionist. Feel into your choices to illuminate your path...

What leads you to do something not in your service is your ego. Base your choices on your heartfelt intuition.

My husband Stewart is the most amazing, centered human; he makes a decision at lightning speed and never goes back. He's confident in his decisions and his career flourishes.

Of course, marrying the right woman helped!

Most of us think that happiness is a someday goal. I used to think that I had to be everything to everybody. My life was not really mine until it dawned upon me that I could fully embrace joy NOW. Radically allowing yourself to be you brings out your true self, filled to the brim with gratitude.

You've got this!

Here are some daily tips, that have helped me centre myself toward success...

Meditation to me is like doing sit-ups. I have a twice-daily practice with remarkable results.

Spray your favourite scent into the air and step through the mist. Focus on a grounded, calm feeling and listen for the signals.

Breathe in for a count of 4 and out for 4. Do this breathing exercise for 6 weeks to improve your rest and digestion. Listen to the sounds of the ocean.
From my heart to yours. How you do something, is how you do everything; all our interactions with life are a moving mediation in being present.

My wish for you is for you to experiment and explore the new you. Yes, you can be multi-disciplined and successful. Enjoy this reinvention process. Listen to your signals, opportunities, and choices; they often come to you as whispers. Reflect on them. Be vulnerable enough to embrace your radically reinvented life without self-judgment.

**Life is short. Breathe it. Create it. Live it.**

My mission is to take you by the hand and assist you in reinventing yourself from the inside out on purpose, so you can enjoy a life full of freedom.

Be The Light,

Zahrina Robertson. Book Zahrina to speak at your next event.

Chapter 2

# The Power of Rewriting Your Life Story

**Sharlene Licciardello**
*Visionary Author, Life Coach, and
Co-Founder of "Rewrite Your Life Story"*

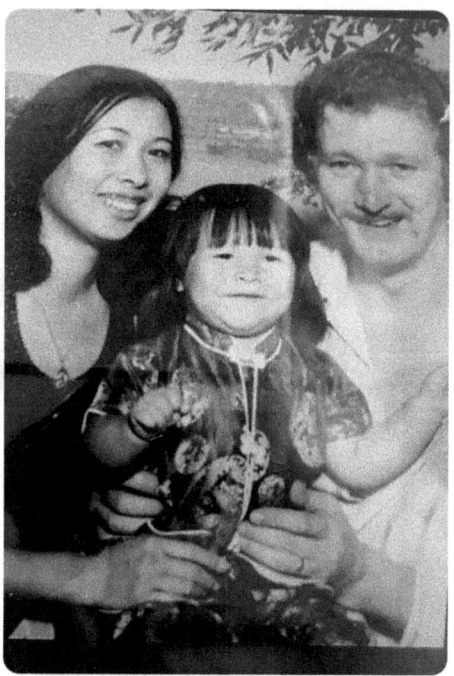

## About the Author: Sharlene Licciardello

Sharlene Licciardello, a visionary author, life coach, and co-founder of "Rewrite Your Life Story," empowers people to reshape their narratives. Her diverse cultural background, blending British and Singaporean roots, embodies resilience, purpose, and storytelling.

Her father's wisdom and mother's loving discipline helped develop Sharlene's character. Early emotional challenges taught Sharlene the value of rewriting personal narratives, and she realised the power of reshaping stories.

Meeting Stephen at 16, Sharlene began a journey of self-improvement. Their teenage love transformed into a lifelong partnership, enriched by their commitment to personal growth. Their pursuit of parenthood through IVF brought heartache, yet with the support of their community, they endured.

Sharlene's experiences led to the "Rewrite Your Life Story" movement, inspiring others to embrace their past, analyse the present, and envision hopeful futures through storytelling. Their podcast became a global beacon for sharing stories of resilience.

Sharlene distilled their journey into Six Pillars for personal growth: Mindset, Self-Awareness, Relationships, Health, Purpose, and Spirituality, providing a remarkable framework for rewriting stories of strength and resilience.

As co-founder of "Rewrite Your Life Story," Sharlene Licciardello empowers individuals to reshape their narratives.

Her legacy is empowerment, believing in everyone's potential to rewrite their life story and thrive.

⬤ ⬤ ⬤ ⬤ ⬤

Life isn't merely a collection of past chapters written in ink; it's also about the inkwell still on your desk, waiting for you to dip your pen into it and write your next sentence. You are the author of this unfolding tale, the keeper of your life's manuscript. With each sunrise, a new page opens up before you, crisp and empty, inviting you to fill it with words, describing your actions and choices that will captivate your audience – and yourself. So why not craft every page so compellingly that it becomes a turning point in your life's story?

Visualise a book. Picture it not as an ordinary book but as a literary masterpiece, bound in exquisite leather, and filled with pages of varying textures. Some pages are drenched in vivid colours, capturing moments of joy, adventure, and triumph. Others are tinged with muted blues and greys, symbolising the trials, doubts, and sorrows that have dotted your timeline. Then, there are the pages still untouched, silently awaiting the stroke of your pen.

Those empty pages? They're your future, ripe with potential, offering endless possibilities for you to script your narrative. The chapters you've already written, whether coloured with pride or regret, are not the final word, far from it.

In this ongoing narrative that is your life, you wield the pen. And with this pen, you own an incredible power to rewrite, reframe, and completely reclaim your story. You can edit the passages that no longer serve you, highlight the lessons you've learned from each trial, and, most importantly, add new chapters that reflect your best version.

So, I ask you, as you hold this pen in your hand, looking at the empty pages that represent the days, months, and years to come, what story will you write? Will you fill these pages with words of empowerment, resilience, and growth, or will you let them be written for you, by circumstance, old patterns, or by the opinion of others? Your life is an unfolding epic that deserves to be both lived and told in a manner that captivates, teaches, and leaves a lasting impression. It's your story. Make it a page-turner!

Imagine a garden that feels like a sanctuary where each flower blooms with innate grace, harmoniously nurtured by the sun, soil, and rain. Envision young Sharlene growing up in an environment equally rich in love and wisdom, a living embodiment of that garden.

I was born to a father from the UK and a mother from Singapore, a union that merged two rich cultures into one. My parents met in Singapore when my father was posted there with the Royal British Air Force. For him, it was love at first sight. My mother, however, needed a little more convincing. Eventually, love blossomed between them, much like the most glorious flowers in that serene garden I want you to picture. They migrated to Australia, married, and soon after, were filled with joyous expectations for the arrival of their first and only child – me.

Growing up, I was the hybrid of two diverse worlds, weaving a tapestry between my father's British legacy and my Singaporean mother's rich culture. I felt immense pride in the duality of my heritage, embracing Asian culinary delights as enthusiastically as the British literature that filled our home.

My father was my gentle mentor; his wisdom was always delivered in strong, yet soft-spoken words. He was the kind and gentle force that fuelled my curiosity and taught me to explore life's deeper meanings. And my mother? She was a strong fortress, a pillar of relentless strength, discipline, and warmth. Her love enveloped us like a cosy blanket, her presence a steadfast assurance that our home was a sanctuary despite the tumultuous world outside. Together, they taught me the value of kindness in word and deed, delivered with grace and humility.

However, life outside this sanctuary had many tumultuous storms. My adolescent years were particularly turbulent. I experienced my fair share of emotional highs and lows, moments when I felt utterly disconnected from the world around me. The school was a battlefield, where I faced not the blatant, in-your-face type of bullying but rather the subtle, insidious kind – nasty, veiled comments and actions aimed to erode my self-worth if I allowed them to.

Lessons of strength, kindness, and individuality that I gleaned from both parents served as a buffer during such hard times in school. They enabled me, from a young age, to learn how to respectfully stand up for myself and be just as comfortable in my own company, as I was with friends. Of course, as a young teenager, I still experienced moments where I would like to fit in and be popular or not face mean comments. After all, I am human. I just knew that at the end of the day, I had a safe place to come back to.

On reflection, I see that each experience, whether pleasant or challenging, contributed to shaping the person I've become. These early life encounters with emotional and psychological hurdles gave me an intuitive understanding of human emotions. I realised that our internal narratives are not fixed scripts but dynamic stories that we can edit and rewrite. My resilience isn't just a trait; it is an inkwell of strength, always available to me when revising a challenging chapter in my life story.

So here's what I want you to remember: just like that serene garden, your life can flourish and evolve, nurtured by your experiences and choices. Understand that past experiences may set the scene, but they do not have the final say over your future. Your resilience is your secret ink, and it's never too late to rewrite your life story, one chapter at a time.

When I first met Stephen, I was just 16, navigating the convoluted labyrinth of teenage years. He was two years my junior, a 14-year-old filled with a contagiously uplifting enthusiasm. Our connection was instant, fortified by youthful exuberance and a deep-seated desire for self-improvement and personal development. Even at that young age, we knew we were kindred spirits, bound by a shared ambition to make the most of our lives and help others.

We decided to cement our commitment when I was 23 and Stephen was 21. Marrying young may have its critics, but for us, it meant that we grew up together – emotionally, intellectually, and spiritually. Every obstacle we faced, and every joy we celebrated, became chapters in a love story that we co-authored from a tender age. Our commitment to each other enriched our journey into adulthood and the process of becoming the best versions of ourselves. Personal development wasn't just a phase or a hobby; it was our lifestyle, imbued into the very fabric of our relationship.

But our narrative took a challenging turn as we embarked on one of the most emotionally demanding journeys a couple can face – the path to parenthood via in vitro fertilisation (IVF). We endured 18 gruelling cycles of IVF, each attempt amassing layers of hope, followed by the soul-crushing disappointment of either a negative result or, worse, another miscarriage. To say the process was an emotional rollercoaster would be a staggering understatement. It was more like a relentless tide, oscillating between the shores of hope and despair, with each ebbing wave erasing our footsteps in the sand as if mocking our efforts.

Complicating matters further was the difficult revelation that Stephen couldn't have children. The news was a heavy blow, adding another layer of complexity to an already intricate challenge. We pressed on and the search for a suitable donor became a medical procedure and a personal quest. We waded through profiles, medical histories, and countless consultations. Each potential match brought a flurry of questions – "Would this donor be the right fit for us? How would this choice shape our future family?"

Though we faced multiple miscarriages, each loss carved out a deeper chamber in our hearts for the children we yearned for. With every setback, our resolve solidified, forming an unbreakable bond that was less about shared success and more about mutual resilience. Our dream of having a family became a pilgrimage, a sacred journey imbued with lessons that no book or seminar could impart.

As we navigated this harrowing path, our community – our tribe – became our sanctuary. The support of family and friends provided much-needed emotional sustenance, serving as a poignant reminder that life's most challenging journeys are not meant to be walked alone. This experience, as agonising as it was, made us realise the absolute necessity of a supportive community that shares in your sorrows just as readily as it celebrates your joys.

In every essence, our struggle with IVF and infertility became an integral part of who we are as individuals and as a couple. It shaped our perspectives on life, resilience, and the human capacity for enduring love. We may not have welcomed a child into our family as we had envisioned, but this chapter, as heart-wrenching as it was, instilled in us a level of empathy and understanding that we could not have gained otherwise.

As we continue on our life's journey, we do so with a deeper appreciation for each other, fortified by the trials and lessons we've endured. That chapter may not have unfolded as we initially imagined. Nonetheless, it's part of our story – a testament to enduring love, resilient spirit, and the untold strength within us all.

The toll of 18 cycles of IVF had worn us down – emotionally, physically, and spiritually. But the defining moment came with an almost surreal finality during that last cycle. Having harvested eight eggs, we were cautiously optimistic. Yet, when the call came through, informing us that none of the eight were viable for transfer, the weight of the news was utterly crushing. At that moment, my body and mind signalled that enough was enough. We knew it was time to step back, to grieve, and to reevaluate the course of our lives.

So, we retreated from the world into our own little haven. We paused our much-loved training sessions, workshops, and speaking engagements. It was a sabbatical not just from work but from the weight of expectations and timelines. This period was vital for us to process our sorrow, honour our grief, and understand that we had reached an existential crossroads. We faced a pivotal choice: childless by nature or childless by choice. We chose the latter, deciding to seize control of our narrative and life's story.

Light began to shine in our hearts during these moments of seclusion and introspection. We found solace in the stories of others – countless narratives brimming with resilience, strength, and transformation. As we listened to these tales, we recognised the universal power of storytelling. Something that has been stitched into the very fabric of humanity, across all cultures throughout the centuries. People from all walks of life were rewriting their narratives, and in doing so, they were shining a light into their dark corners, as well as ours.

Our most enlightened vision emerged from this period of profound darkness: "Rewrite Your Life Story." It became more than a campaign; it evolved into a movement. Our mission aimed to inspire individuals to consider their pasts, analyse their present and look toward their futures with lenses tinted by hope, compassion, and wonder. While unique to us, we understood that our story shared a common thread, as everyone has personal chapters they wish to rewrite. "Rewrite Your Life Story" was conceived as a supportive space for people to reclaim the power in their life story, foster resilience, and become catalysts for positive change.

Can you envision it? A global community where everyone's rewritten story serves as a beacon of hope for someone else who may be drifting in the turbulent seas of life. By launching this movement, we didn't just discover a new sense of purpose; we discovered our life's calling. We began seeing our world as a vibrant landscape painting, bursting with colours of endless and untapped potential.

The trials we endured laid the cornerstone for this movement, allowing us to channel our experiences into a transformative and empowering platform.

Our past struggles are now strong cords woven into the fabric of this initiative, committing us to helping others reclaim and rewrite their own life stories. It's a cause deeply rooted in our journey – a testament to the courageous, ever-growing human spirit and the transformative power of storytelling.

Launching our podcast was like flinging open grand gates to a vibrant global community. It felt as though we invited the world into the cosy, warm space of our living room, where an atmosphere of vulnerability, courage, and wisdom thrived. Our microphone transformed from mere technology to a conduit connecting souls across continents and cultures.

Each episode unfolded like a chapter in an epic novel, brimming with the raw beauty and complexity of the human experience. Every interview resonated as an affirmation of humanity's indomitable spirit, echoing across airwaves and into the hearts and minds of our listeners. From awe-inspiring accounts of overcoming seemingly insurmountable obstacles to spellbinding narratives of life-altering transformations, our podcast wove together a rich tapestry of resilience, courage, and the unyielding drive to flourish.

But what moved us were the life lessons we gleaned from our guests. Every conversation opened a new realm of understanding and perspective. Each story, though unique in its own way, led us back to a profound commonality. When asked, "If you could rewrite your life story, what would it look like?" the answer came in many forms but the theme was universal – "I wouldn't change a thing; my story has made me who I am today."

It was a revelation, a testament to the notion that our past struggles and challenges, however brutal they may seem, contribute to the richness of our characters and the depths of our souls. It was a lesson in embracing authenticity and the full spectrum of the human experience – be it joy, sorrow, or anything in between.

Our podcast matured into far more than a platform; it evolved into an illuminating beacon for those lost in the abyss of life's challenges. It served as a gentle push for individuals teetering on the edges of monumental life shifts, as a sanctuary for those needing solace, and for others as a celebration of life in all its glory and the joy of cheering for the many courageous guests who shared their stories of transformation. In essence, it became a living, breathing embodiment of the power of a supportive community and the incredible resilience that springs from collective human experience.

This realisation was both humbling and uplifting in equal measure, reinforcing our belief in the mission of "Rewrite Your Life Story." It reaffirmed that stories are not merely tales to be told but powerful tools for transformation – a belief we continue to champion as we write new chapters in this extraordinary journey.

Life is a complex narrative with twists and turns that can propel you toward growth or set you back. At "Rewrite Your Life Story", our philosophy is grounded in the conviction that everyone has the agency to actively edit, revise, and rewrite their life's narrative. Whether starting a new chapter or revising an old one, the core principle remains the same: you are the author of your life.

Our journey has led us through a labyrinth of challenges and triumphs, beginning in our youth as teenage sweethearts and continuing through the trials we've faced. These experiences prompted us to conceptualize the process of rewriting life as an active, conscious, and transformative endeavour. To simplify this intricate journey, we've distilled it into six foundational pillars. These pillars are not merely recommendations; they are the structural beams that uphold the framework of a reimagined life.

### The Six Pillars Unveiled: Mindset, Self-Awareness, Relationships, Health, Purpose, and Spirituality

**Pillar One: Mindset - The Lens Through Which You See Your Story**

Our first pillar underscores the importance of adopting a growth mindset. While a fixed mindset can be limiting, a growth mindset liberates you. This pillar encourages embracing a perspective that views challenges as tools for personal sculpting, chiselling you into an improved version of yourself. With this mindset, you become the hero and narrator of your own story and the resources to help you make your own life better become more clear to you.

*Pillar Two: Self-Awareness - The Author's Note to Self*

The second pillar revolves around self-awareness, serving as your internal editor. To rewrite your life story, you must intimately understand your strengths, weaknesses, values, and aspirations. This self-awareness informs your choices and directs your path.

*Pillar Three: Relationships - The Supporting Characters in Your Narrative*

Life isn't a solitary journey; it is a collaborative effort filled with interactions and experiences with other people. This pillar emphasizes the value of nurturing relationships that enrich your soul, stimulate your mind, and elevate your narrative with a deeper sense of meaning. It also emphasizes the importance of distancing yourself from toxic relationships that can hinder your growth.

*Pillar Four: Health - The Physical Manuscript of Your Being*

Your body and mind serve as the parchment and ink of your life story. By nurturing your physical and mental health, you ensure the durability and quality of the pages upon which your narrative unfolds. Health isn't merely an act of maintenance but a profound act of self-respect for the temple that is your body.

*Pillar Five: Purpose - The Plot That Drives Your Story*

Purpose forms the central plotline of your life's novel. This pillar guides you towards aligning your narrative with a purpose that transcends your individual self, creating ripples of positive impact. It encourages you to align your goals and actions with your purpose and regularly evaluate your progress.

*Pillar Six: Spirituality - The Epilogue That Never Ends*

Your life story doesn't conclude in the final chapter; it continues through spirituality, providing a larger context and deeper understanding of your life's experiences. Spirituality opens you up to intangible elements, whether they be through faith, mindfulness, or a connection with nature, offering a broader perspective on your narrative. It is a nurturing practice that connects you with something greater than yourself and enriches the ongoing epilogue of your life story.

The tapestry of your life is woven, supported by the framework of these six pillars. As you engage with each one, you gain the skills, wisdom, and courage to edit, adjust and rewrite whole chapters of your life story. It's an ongoing process, and Stephen and I are committed to guiding you through every sentence, paragraph, and chapter yet to be written.

I always ask our podcast guests: "What would you do if you could rewrite your life story?" For me, the answer is crystal clear – I wouldn't change a thing.

Each trial and triumph have served as a memorable ink stroke that carefully designed the woman I am today.

Imagine your life as an unfolding bestseller, packed with chapters of heartache and happiness, pitfalls, and peaks. But remember this: you're not just the main character in this story. You are its author, and with that pen, you can edit, revise, and write new chapters that resonate with your authentic self. It's a journey that's not just about you; it also empowers those around you, creating a ripple effect, a legacy of inspiration and change.

In the "Rewrite Your Life Story" community, we offer more than just words – we provide the tools, support, and inspiration to turn your life's story into your life's work. Your story is your legacy. So, here's to rewriting, revising, and, most importantly, living your life story – one empowering chapter at a time. Life is waiting for your imprint; let's make it a bold one.

rewriteyourlifestory.com.au

Connect with me

Chapter 3

# Madame Butterfly – Living with Disability

**Jackie Breasley**
*Global Keynote Speaker, Disability Thought Leader and Author*

## About The Author: Jackie Breasley

Jackie Breasley is a Keynote Speaker, thought leader and author. She has lived experience of physical and sensory disabilities, experience navigating the NDIS, and has worked in the disability sector in a variety of roles for 12 years. Some of the interesting and more unusual projects Jackie has worked on include the Disability Access and Inclusion Plan for Fremantle Prison and the social enterprise start-up "B-Hart" both of which have benefited from her passion for advocating for a human rights model of disability. She is also undertaking a Masters of Disability Practice and Leadership at Flinders University and is a member of her Local Council's access and inclusion advisory committee.

Jackie's story is topical and important, with the Royal Commission into Violence, Abuse, Neglect and Exploitation of People with Disability highlighting the need for systemic and cultural change.

Jackie tells her story to illustrate the importance of disability awareness and a human rights approach. Through raising awareness, Jackie hopes to inspire positive change for people with disability and more inclusive communities. She is obsessed with lending her voice to enshrining the human rights of people with disability.

Jackie is married, with one fur baby, a massive INXS fan, and is still celebrating Collingwood's 2023 Grand Final victory!

• • • • •

If we were all the same, life would be boring. If I had a dollar for every time I've been told, "**Good things come in small packages**," or a child reacted in wonderment or bewilderment ("*That's a small lady, Mum!*") at seeing me, I'd be rich!

I am writing my story to raise awareness of Turner Syndrome and to highlight the importance of the United Nations Convention on the Rights of People with Disability (UNCRPD) and the Human Rights Model of Disability.

**Models of Disability**

There have been several models of disability throughout history with the main four being the charity model, the medical model, the social model, and most recently, the human rights model of disability. The charity model is based on the religious belief that people with disability need charity and "looking after". The medical model is based on the premise that the person with disability is broken and needs medical intervention to be fixed. More recently, the social model is based on the belief that society, and particularly the built environment, is the cause of inequality. Fixing that will enable people with disability to lead normal lives.

The human rights model of disability, however, recognises that it is more than the built environment that stops people with disability from leading a good life. The human rights model embraces disability as a normal part of the human condition, recognises people with disability as experts in all things that affect them, and makes governments accountable for taking action to protect the human rights of people with disability.

As the recent Royal Commission has highlighted, and research compiled in the Australian Institute of Health and Welfare's People with Disability 2022 report tells us, one in six, or approximately **4.4 million Australians** has a disability. People of working age with disability have a 48% employment rate compared with 80% for those without disability. Shockingly, 47% of people with disability have experienced violence after the age of 15.

How can we achieve an inclusive society where people with disability have choice and control and systems are challenged to enable people with disability to participate socially and economically as far as possible? By teaching disability awareness in school, making disability mainstream in the media, showing how people with disability can live good lives with the right technology and support, but most of all involving people with disability in designing systems and making decisions that impact their lives.

**My Diagnosis**

The journey to my diagnosis was long. I was wearing glasses by 18 months of age, had eight teeth removed to accommodate my small jaw, and had an operation to tighten my eye muscle by the age of five. That same year, I was sent home from primary school with a letter recommending I see a paediatrician as I was not hitting developmental milestones. I already had a sense of being different but not in the way I hope we embrace difference today. The human rights model of disability recognises difference as part of the human experience and acknowledges that we all have basic human rights.

Finally, at age seven, and after numerous tests, I was diagnosed with Turner Syndrome. I remember the unmistakable smell of antiseptic and a man with long hair running several tests at the Royal Children's Hospital to check on my kidneys and other vital organs whilst I tried to maintain my modesty.

According to the Mayo Clinic, Turner Syndrome affects only females and results when one of the X or sex chromosomes is missing or partially missing. Evidence from various sources including the Royal Children's Hospital and the American Academy of Family Physicians shows that Turner Syndrome occurs in about **1:2500 live births, with 98 to 99% of pregnancies aborted or resulting in stillbirth.**

Turner Syndrome causes a variety of medical and developmental problems with the most notable including short stature, ovarian dysgenesis or failure of the ovaries, and heart defects. Women with Turner Syndrome are unable to produce their own estrogen or progesterone. Hearing difficulties, kidney issues, and autoimmune disease are among some of the complications which are possible, along with the aforementioned vision and jaw issues.

The clinical features of Turner Syndrome that contribute to the wonderful richness of human difference include:

- Wide or weblike neck
- Low-set ears
- Broad chest with widely spaced nipples
- High, narrow roof of the mouth (palate)
- Arms that turn outward at the elbows
- Fingernails and toenails that are narrow and turned upward
- Swelling of the hands and feet, especially at birth
- Slightly smaller than average height at birth
- Low hairline at the back of the head
- Receding or small lower jaw
- Short fingers and toes
- Melanocytic nevi (raised moles)

When I was diagnosed, there were not many treatment options available. My parents were told I had a life expectancy of 40 and they went away for a few days to absorb the news. My sister and I stayed with my godparents, and I tried to be so good. I didn't really understand why my parents went away but I knew it was my fault.

At the age of ten, my paediatrician (a white middle-aged male) told me that I would not be able to have children. I asked, "Should I tell him he's adopted, then?" which left the paediatrician dumbfounded. I had the obligatory tests and went home. My father knelt to my level and asked if I understood. I said I did because I had already figured out for myself that I was too small to successfully carry a child, so it was no surprise when the paediatrician told me I wouldn't have children.

It was not until the age of fifteen that I met another Turner woman for the first time, thanks to the epically titled article, **"The Gene Mistake"** in the local paper. I soon met more Turner women and participated in running the Victorian Turner Syndrome Association. This was my first taste of organised activity to improve the quality of our lives. We enjoyed some great times together with lots of social functions that were full of laughter and noise. We are small but we are loud!

There were also several discussions about the "Turner look". At that time there was, for most of us in the group of Turner teens, a hate-hate relationship with the clinical features that combined to create what we called the "Turner look". The moles, webbed skin, low-set ears and hairline, and curled nails were agonised over, and we wanted the medical model of disability to fix us, as we felt we were "broken".

The following year, my family moved house, and this meant moving schools. For me, this involved moving from a girls' school to a co-ed school. Hard enough at that age when all you want to do is be the same as everyone else, but I had also made the decision to stop growth medication and begin hormone replacement therapy to mimic puberty. I moved school around the time the effects of my hormone therapy were becoming apparent, making me agonisingly self-conscious.

This is about the time that I experienced physical and emotional bullying that has stayed with me to this day. At that time, there was no recognition of human rights, no bullying policies in schools, and certainly no understanding of the terrible consequences of bullying. I was thrown against a locker, pelted with fruit, or, my personal favourite, my peers wanting to put me in a microwave. None of that compares to this moment in time that I still recall clearly today. It was a warm day, and we were in our awful green and brown summer uniform, about to endure a Year 11 economics class. As there were only six to eight of us brave and crazy enough to take Year 11 economics, the class was held in a tiny meeting room off the school library. There were four tables arranged in a square, so we were essentially all at the same table.

Our teacher, Mrs Mazzer, went out of the room for some reason. The next thing I knew, I was surrounded and being asked by girls from the popular "it" group, "Do you have a boyfriend?", "Have you kissed?", "Have you had sex?" and "Did you use a condom?" All the while, the girl next to me was rubbing her school shoes up and down my bare legs. It was incredibly intimidating, and I felt physically vulnerable. As soon as the class was over, I bolted for the toilets with my best friend in hot pursuit. She wanted to get me out of there before the "it" group came in for their daily smoke.

Can you imagine what that felt like for a sixteen-year-old who was still getting used to her changing body? I was totally humiliated and traumatised – it cut me to the core. I remember going to the sick bay and the Year Coordinator was called. One look into my terrified eyes and I was sent home. The "it" group was clearly reprimanded and they were overly nice to me from that point on.

All this had me thinking about quitting school. To their credit, Mum and Dad let me make my own decision. Eventually, I decided that I would be giving the "it" group too much power in my life if I retreated and so I completed year 12, albeit using a punishing study schedule to cope. I needed to find my voice and stand up for my rights and staying in school helped me become stronger and more resilient.

As I moved into my late teens and early twenties, I found my body image and self-esteem at rock bottom. I was emotionally eating, and I really needed someone to talk to. I spoke to my specialist who referred me to a counsellor. It's a measure of how far I've come that during those sessions my counsellor decided to have me keep a diary as I couldn't express myself adequately. Handing over that diary every fortnight was the most excruciating yet liberating feeling!

Around this time, I also had my appendix removed. A routine procedure. It was only at my check-up after the procedure that the surgeon (again, a white middle-aged male) announced that he'd taken the opportunity to have a look at my ovaries whilst they were operating. That is not a big deal except that I was not shown the respect of being asked beforehand. I did not consent to it, I did not ask the surgeon to check my ovaries and he did not ask permission to do so. My human rights were considered less important than his medical curiosity. There have been several instances where the medical model of disability (where we are perceived as broken and in need of fixing) has positioned me and others with disability as objects of curiosity, not humans with rights, rather like a circus animal.

I'm not sure what made me think that the minute I finished high school I would not be bullied anymore. Such naivety would not go unpunished. I either let it go or tried to sort out situations one-on-one. In the end, I moved jobs, jumping from the frying pan into the fire. Your position becomes untenable when you are accidentally copied in on an email that is denigrating you or when you are leading a project and can't trust the others in the team working with you.

In the mid-1990s, I was retrenched from my job. I got a harsh lesson in why only 48% of people with disability have a job. I was told I was the successful applicant for a job and then about an hour later told I wasn't. I screamed into the phone at the outplacement provider who later told me that it was fine; he just sat at his desk with his feet up while I vented! I had told Mum and Dad that I had found a job and it was just awful having to explain that actually, I didn't.

The loss of that job ended up leading to a meeting with my namesake Scobie Breasley. Scobie was a famous jockey in his day who won five Caulfield Cups. The best and fairest prize for jockeys is named the Scobie Breasley medal. The landline (yes, we still had them then) rang one day in response to an ad I had put in the local paper (I'm really aging myself, aren't I!). "It's Arthur Breasley here," the caller announced in his very English accent. I established it was

Scobie and went to his magnificent mansion full of racing memorabilia to do some administrative assistant work for him. He took one look at me and said, **"You should have been a jockey!"** I couldn't make that up if I tried and it's definitely a true story!

I have now been working in the broader community services sector for 13 years and the disability sector for 12 years. It is only since working in the disability sector that I feel acknowledged, understood, and at home. I would not be comfortable working in any other sector now and it feels like home because I have found my purpose.

I knew from a young age that I was not going to have children, however, with advances in IVF it became possible for women with Turner Syndrome to have children with a donated egg. I couldn't bear to accept that I might now be able to have children, in case that was taken away from me again. The reality in my case was that the risk of aortic dissection, or a tear in the inner layer of the aorta, was too great. I also had not met anyone I wanted to raise children with!

That changed when I met my wonderful husband 15 years ago. It put infertility firmly back on my radar as an issue. My husband is from China and as our relationship became more serious, I called in our future best man to help. Yes, I explained to my future husband that I have Turner Syndrome and cannot have children, with our future best man acting as interpreter! This is a man who pretended to forget the ring on our wedding day as a joke!

Soon after, I received the last pair of hearing aids Job Access approved. Hearing loss is a clinical feature of Turner Syndrome that not all women experience but I am as deaf as a post! Even now I am reluctant to wear my hearing aids. This is partly denial and partly because they are just so damn uncomfortable! Hearing loss is a barrier to relating with other people and is incredibly frustrating and isolating. It is also very annoying for my work colleagues, family, and friends. These days I can barely have a conversation with my husband across the dinner table without needing my hearing aids. Don't get me started on trying to communicate during COVID with everyone wearing masks!

**Finding My Why**

So, what does the future hold, and where I am at now? As my sister so eloquently put it, I wear the chip on my shoulder with a little more grace these days. Time is a wonderful healer and provider of perspective. Every now and again, we all need to take stock and have a look in the mirror.

This is a journal entry from early 2022 which I wrote while on a retreat with a note to myself:

For perhaps the first time last night I felt like I was really strong and just went with it.

Yet I still feel like I have some kind of moral obligation to hate my body because I do not fit society's expectations.

I am very connected to my body this morning and feeling every niggle, every pain point. Also feeling quite raw and tears are streaming down my face as I write.

But %^&% I also feel so fierce and in no mood to curl up. I fought so hard just to survive so wanna talk moral obligation – live your life and maybe try to be gentle.

Turner Syndrome is a big part of who I am, and it has given me my purpose in life for the last 12 to 13 years. Most of all I give thanks that I am one of the lucky 1-2% with Turner Syndrome that survived to full term. I have learned empathy, resilience, and determination (some may say stubbornness). When I was younger, I would have given anything to be "normal" whatever that is. Now I would not change having Turner Syndrome and not change being me.

My purpose is to advance disability awareness and human rights for people with disability. I want to live my life and stop playing small. I am currently enrolled in a Masters of Disability Practice and Leadership at Flinders University and look forward to continuing my studies next year. I am also on the Access & Inclusion Committee of my local council. I invite you to find out more about me and share your experiences by visiting my website and connecting with me on LinkedIn, Facebook, or Instagram.

One of my favourite songs by Australian band INXS is 'The Stairs' which expresses how all of us are great, even though we are different. It identifies the need for passion and purpose in our lives, and I believe this has been true for me. We are all different, yet we all deserve dignity and the same human rights, and I'm doing my part to make that a reality.

*There are reasons here to give your life*
*And follow in your way*
*The passion lives to keep your faith*
*Though all are different, all are great*
*Climbing as we fall*
*We dare to hold on to our fate*
*And steal away our destiny*
*To catch ourselves with quiet grace*

The Stairs, Andrew Farriss, and the late, great Michael Hutchence of INXS.

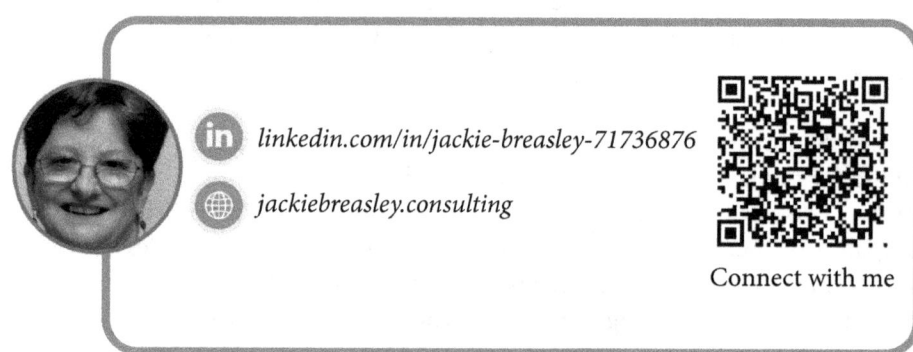

linkedin.com/in/jackie-breasley-71736876

jackiebreasley.consulting

Connect with me

Chapter 4

# Rise, Woman, Rise - Finding Your "Eye of The Tiger"

**Jo Worthy**
*Global Keynote Speaker, Founder of the Worthy Women Movement, and Author*

## About The Author: Jo Worthy

Jo Worthy is the founder of the **Worthy Women Movement**, author of "Love Worthy – 21 Lessons in Creating A Deliciously Divine Life" and a contributing author in four collaborative books. Jo mentors authors, coaches and healers to become more **visible, courageous, self-confident** and **creative** so that they can **RISE** into their **greatness**.

Jo is a motivational speaker, specialising in **COURAGE** and also has an absolute passion for womens retreats, running both 'The Bali Bliss Retreat' and 'Master Your Signature Talk' Retreat'.

Under Jo's initiative, a yearly Worthy Women EmPOWERment Conference is held. The vision of the Movement is also expanding with the creation of The Speaker Hub and Worthy Women Online Summits starting in 2024. The Movement also provides co-author opportunities, with the latest project "Rising in Worth, Wealth & Wisdom" due for release in 2024.

Jo believes wholeheartedly that stories are the catalyst to real change and an inspiration to take action. She knows that speaking is one of the most powerful ways to be able to share your story, wisdom, knowledge and expertise and be an inspiration to many.

To book a motivational speaker who specialises in helping people step into their courage and find their 'eye of the tiger', contact jo@worthywomenmovement.com. Jo will enhance your event by motivating your guests with her high energy, authentic and impactful delivery and unique approach.

• • • • •

Bullied, isolated and abused. For many years, I suffered in school, the workplace, and at home. As a woman I have been abused emotionally, physically, sexually, and also financially. I have attracted people and intense situations that have taught me the harshest of lessons and at times it was really tough to keep going. My journey to finding my inner strength, my 'eye of the tiger' has been immense, with so many obstacles, fears and adversity to overcome. Since my childhood, I felt disconnected, alone, and lacking self-confidence. I constantly lived in fear of being rejected and not feeling good enough. Bullying and all forms of abuse can take its toll on you and flatten your spirit so much that you can lose sight of all that greatness within and it can be a long road back to liking yourself, never mind loving and appreciating yourself.

Yet my story is one of encouragement, hope and resilience. It's a story of never giving up, even when I felt that the odds were stacked against me. It's about getting up when I felt defeated, failing, stupid and fearful. It's a story of courage, as I frequently forced myself out of my comfort zone, stretching myself to uncover those gifts within me that were so deeply buried and neglected.

I often felt a failure and wondered what on earth I was doing with my life. I relied too much on what other people thought of me, desperately wanting their validation and acceptance, however, many of these people did not have my best interests at heart. Instead, I second-guessed myself, I did not trust in my intuition and I certainly didn't back myself. My self-confidence hit rock bottom many times and I lost my way, numbing out my pain with sex, food, shopping, and gambling. All of my incredible creativity and talents lay dormant, forgotten and neglected for many years.

If I was going to strive towards reaching my full potential, I knew that I had to make some massive changes. Starting in my early 20s, I worked tirelessly on my spiritual and personal development. I invested heavily in myself and my business and I was determined to become a far better version of myself. Many times, I felt like I was going around in circles, not really getting anywhere, taking one step forward and three steps backwards. I encountered many curve balls and climbed the toughest of mountains and yet eventually I came out the other side, stronger, wiser and proud of myself for reaching a new level of growth and expansion.

I understand that some of you will not resonate with the pain of bullying, abuse and addiction, however many of you will relate to the feelings of low self-worth and lacking self-confidence. My wish is that you find your 'eye of the tiger', rising into your most incredible version, becoming more visible, creative and reigniting your passion for your life and your business. I want to see you become bold and brave as you strive towards your greatness.

**Say what you want to say, allowing those words to fall out freely!**

**I want to see you be COURAGEOUS!**

This is my story of how I was able to step fully into my courage many times and finally be able to 'say what I want to say and allow my words to fall out' after many years of self-doubt and insecurity. I had to stop living in the past, concentrate on the present and plan for my future. I had to change old paradigms, negative conditioning and beliefs.

Allow me to take you back to how I felt as a young girl. I was not popular at school and I was labelled a 'dag' and was often the target of severe bullying. I felt like I didn't have a voice, and as the youngest sibling growing up, I felt I was seen as stupid and ugly.

I was bullied at school by my so-called 'friends' and both my sister and I were bullied quite badly by our older brother, who was verbally and physically abusive, dealing with his own fears which played out aggressively. I lacked any self-confidence and the courage to stand up for myself. I feared the dark and thought there were monsters in my bedroom! Unfortunately, the bullying and sexual harassment would also continue into my work life and it was going to become a pattern that I needed to clear if I really wanted to rise.

Growing up, we lived in the worst house in the street and I was lucky to get a new dress and one pair of shoes for the year and this attracted more bullying. The fact that I wore very thick glasses all the way through primary school and most of high school didn't help! Kids can be so bloody cruel! Mum and Dad had their own issues and separated when I was 11, but I was lucky in the sense that I still felt loved by both my parents and I was grateful that I had a creative spirit. I was better off than some children – at least I had a roof over my head, a bed to sleep in, some clothes, lovely meals cooked and parents who loved me, even if they didn't love each other very much.

I took comfort in creativity, writing plays from the age of four and performing whenever I could. In those moments I was in not in fear and it was pure joy. When I was just playing myself, Jo, I was a fearful, insecure girl who would continue many of her ingrained patterns and behaviours into adulthood. I was the nervous girl who just wanted to fade away into the background, yet unfortunately I was so short-sighted I had to sit up the front of the classroom. Unless I was writing or performing, I was tremendously shy and insecure, and I couldn't even put up my hand to ask a question, I was that fearful! I didn't ask questions and suffered in silence.

Throughout my life I continued to surround myself in fear. Fearful of the judgments from others, fearful of criticism, worrying whether I was liked and accepted. I feared being rejected and ridiculed and I questioned whether I was really good enough – at anything! I never felt proud of anything that I had done and often wished I was someone else. My life was very mediocre in many ways, lacking direction, stability and I certainly wasn't living courageously or creatively. Deep within those intricate layers my sad heart and soul craved so much more.

As I got into my teens and my adulthood, I forgot about the very things that gave me lots of joy. Fast-forward to my mid-40s, I started to realise I had very little self-confidence and I second-guessed everything about myself, settling on mediocrity, which included my relationships, the jobs I accepted and my friendships. My self-worth seemed non-existent at times and it was going to be a long journey back to connecting to my greatness within. I certainly was not striving towards my highest potential. Actually, it was quite the reverse and this was played out in dramatic ways.

The journey was going to be a long one, as old patterns and negative conditioning can be challenging to change and it's not until we become consciously aware of these patterns that we can start the road back to more joy, peace and confidence. In my 20s, I started learning about the Law of Attraction and I learnt how powerful our minds can be. I started on my journey to improving my mindset and the language I used towards myself and others. As I reflect back on those times, I see various times I was going way off track and I actually now realise that I had very harsh, yet valuable lessons to learn.

I began a pattern of attracting toxic relationships in all forms and unfortunately attracted three abusive relationships. The second relationship was very severe as I was abused in every way and I was in such a mess emotionally afterwards, I did not know how I would survive. The fact that I had a mother and a stepfather who loved me unconditionally and a four-year old daughter to raise without her father, was all that kept me going.

My next relationship would be with one of the most caring, loving and affectionate men that I could wish for (except for my very first love at 15!). However, it was an old pattern to reject any healthy relationship as I didn't feel worthy of it, and after three years I left and plunged head-on into another abusive relationship. This one was particularly abusive verbally, until after two failed attempts, I managed to leave. He stalked me and threatened my life. It was at this point I declared something very powerful:

> I WAS DONE! I was done with the abuse.
>
> I WAS DONE with living in mediocrity.
>
> I WAS DONE with suffering.
>
> I WAS DONE with living in misery.

I started to feel that there was a glimmer of hope as I recognised that I deserved a lot better. I began connecting deeply to that 'warrior woman' within and even though I was being manipulated and threatened, I had had enough! My fearless warrior switch was turned on.

Within 12 months of my 'I am done' declaration I would meet my Mr. Worthy and we eventually get married in 2017. How ironic that I could spend my entire life up to that point searching for self-worth and then I meet and marry my Mr. Worthy! Life works in incredible ways.

**FEEL THE FEAR AND DO IT REGARDLESS!**

It was when my Mr. Worthy and I were sharing our lives and our dreams together that I started to run a business whilst I was also working full-time. I invested heavily in my business development, joining high-level coaching programs and going to many conferences, seminars, and retreats. I was a woman who feared public speaking more than death itself and was around this time that I decided to set myself a challenge and that was to put my hand up to ask a question at every event. This does not seem a lot to some, but for someone who feared public speaking and didn't even put up her hand to ask questions throughout her life, it was huge for me.

In 2016, my Mr. Worthy and I went to Bali, which would end up being one of the most profound trips of my life. I started to reactivate my passion for creativity, and I began writing my first book, Love Worthy. It took me four years to finish this book, in between working and running a business, but I was determined to finish. I was about to publish my book Love Worthy at the end of 2019 when I got into a state of fear, thinking OMG, I cannot publish this book! It was so raw, and I started to feel so exposed. I was so scared of being judged and rejected. I had started studying one of the vulnerability experts, Brené Brown, watching her YouTube videos and then I started researching her inspirational quotes. The one that stood out the most and was so relevant to me at this time was:

*"If you are not in the arena getting your arse kicked,
I don't want your feedback."*

**- Brené Brown**

That quote alone quickly changed my attitude and I realised that if others are NOT writing a tell-all memoir that is raw (and juicy in parts), not putting themselves out there and becoming more visible, speaking on stages and stepping deeply into their courage, then I don't want their feedback! It's no surprise that it's most often the ones that are critical and judgemental who are the ones not in the arena! It was at that time that I had a paradigm shift and decided that I would publish Love Worthy.

The irony is that some did reject me. Some 'friends' refused to come to my book launch, and their lack of support was an eye-opener, that's for sure. I worked through my layers and started to heal this old pattern of 'people-pleasing', understanding that not everyone will like me and that is perfectly OK – who cares if others do not like me or my book!

Most of my life I had said YES when I meant NO and I had this deep desire to always be liked and accepted. I feared rejection and judgement from others to the point of dimming myself down, fearful of shining too brightly, fearful of upsetting others and not 'fitting in'. I have felt like the most unpopular person in the universe at times, but I decided to step into my courage time and time again when I did not feel liked or accepted.

## You either like me or you don't!

Guess what? I started to feel this absolute freedom that I had never felt before and I learnt that you can be an amazing human being, and some people still won't like you. This quote resonates so deeply with me and I utilise it during my keynotes:

> "You can be the ripest, juiciest peach in the world and there's still going to be somebody who hates peaches."
>
> **- Dita Von Teese**

I am me and you are you and there is no one like me or you on this planet! We are all unique and to fully claim our power we need to understand this and stop thinking something is wrong with us because we are not liked or accepted. It can take a lot of courage to adopt this attitude and you will have to remain very focussed on your vision and connect deeply to your 'eye of the tiger' to succeed in your business.

> "Today you are You, that is truer than true. There is no-one alive who is YOUER than You!"
>
> **- Dr Suess**

The incredible result of stopping the need to 'people-please' is that it allows us to really start stepping into our brilliance. We can start to uncover all that gold within, layer by layer, step by step. We will also have so much more energy to explore our own greatness when we stop wasting our valuable time and energy worrying about the need to be liked and accepted.

> "Realising you don't need to fit in and you don't have to be liked and accepted by everyone will set you free from your emotional prison."
>
> **- Jo Worthy**

I believe that every single one of us has that warrior within and that no matter what life throws at us, every challenge, betrayal, setback, rejection, perceived failure, is a chance to RISE above! It's a chance to fuel your fire and connect to your 'eye of the tiger', not allowing anyone or anything to take you off your path. This is essential if you are going to fully succeed in your business. Make sure your 'why' is greater than any challenges and keep RISING.

## FIND THAT GRIT AND DETERMINATION WITHIN YOU, YOUR WARRIOR WITHIN AND KEEP RISING!

To keep RISING, you must leave any past misery behind, which includes forgiving yourself and others, refusing to become bitter and disenchanted. Utilise the power of gratitude, for all that you have and all of who you are becoming. Be so proud of the person that you are becoming and acknowledge that you have worked so hard to become the woman that you are today. I want you to be proud, bold and brave!

> *"I am a courageous, confident warrior woman who refuses to quit on herself, or her business and I will unravel my hidden gifts that have been buried deep within me."*
>
> **- Jo Worthy**

Living by these philosophies and constantly stepping into my courage has grown my business, which I started in 2013. It was very challenging at times with many projects failing to convert. However, I kept tweaking and improving with a strong refusal to quit even on my hardest days when I thought everything was going pear-shaped! I had to increase my technical knowledge, work deeply on my belief systems and I stopped the need to be liked and accepted by everyone. I also began to align myself with other incredible people; mentors, friends and clients that were genuinely supportive and who would celebrate my success and not be threatened by it. I had to learn some very harsh lessons, both in my personal life and my business life, to realise that every perceived 'failure' was another stepping-stone towards me rising more into my divine purpose to forge ahead.

I ran my first event in 2014, my first retreat in 2015 and then went on to write and then publish my first solo book, Love Worthy, in 2019. Going back to writing again was one of my biggest joys and opened up a whole new vortex of creativity within me that had laid dormant for so long. After publishing my book, so many other wonderful creative projects were launched, including writing two online programs. I am now a co-author in four books (including this one!). My life has changed in so many miraculous ways as I refused to allow my past fears and insecurities to rule my life and I started to connect back to my courage, creativity and confidence, trusting and listening to myself.

In 2022, I created one of the biggest and boldest projects, The Worthy Women Summit. I knew it was more than just an event and soon a whole movement, the Worthy Women Movement, was birthed! My vision for the Movement is to guide, mentor and inspire women to become more visible, step deeply into their courage, and find their 'eye of the tiger' whilst increasing their self-confidence. I want each woman to follow their divine purpose, with a particular emphasis on authors, speakers and coaches becoming unstoppable in their pursuit of their divine purpose, including sharing their powerful stories, knowledge and wisdom. My life has come full circle, from that scared little girl, to that sad, fearful woman finding her 'eye of the tiger' and becoming unstoppable in her courage, vision and her mission to make a difference. I now mentor other women to become great speakers, and I was once someone who feared public speaking! I now have so many gems to share and help others.

*"Do one thing every day that scares you."*

**- Eleanor Roosevelt**

These days when I look back, I am amazed at what I have encountered and the resilience and the courage it has taken to get to where I am now. I am now passionate about not only my story but every woman's story, as they can be powerful, inspire change and motivate action. My wish is that I can inspire and motivate all that read my story and realise that every single one of us has the potential to step into a better version of ourselves, heal from our past and live a much more rich, empowering and delicious life.

I also know that this is a continuing journey and that I will keep learning, growing and becoming even better as each year goes by; I am on a mission to become my best self in this lifetime. I know that changing my negative conditioning and mindset and old ingrained patterns that were not serving me, were the keys to RISING into my better version. After everything that I have experienced, I am never complacent, and I am so bloody grateful for all that I have and all the incredible people that I have now attracted into my life.

From my heart to yours, my wish is that you become the most amazing version of yourself. I want you to keep rising into your greatness and share all the gifts that you have kept buried deep within your soul. I want you to become the best that you can be. I want you to step up, a bold warrior woman on a mission, totally focussed and in her power. As you heal the layers deep within, you'll RISE above the betrayal, the disappointments, the grief and the perceived failures.

*"Our greatest fear is that we are powerful beyond measure. It is our light, not our darkness, that most frightens us. Who am I to be brilliant, gorgeous, talented, fabulous? Actually, who are you not to be?"*

**- Marianne Williamson**

I want to see you go out into the world and be **fabulous, talented, gorgeous** and **brilliant** as you rise into your courage and become a fearless warrior woman on a mission who has reignited her passion for life and her business. Be a shining star, a beacon of light guiding others to do the same.

Here's to your greatness! **RISE, WOMAN, RISE AND KEEP RISING!**

Jo Worthy x

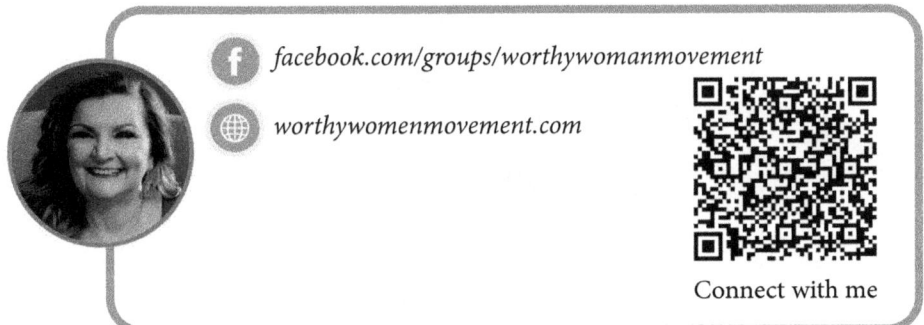

*facebook.com/groups/worthywomanmovement*

*worthywomenmovement.com*

Connect with me

Chapter 5

# Shattering Glass Ceilings: One woman's commitment to empowering women to take their seats at the corporate table

**Rachel Pleasant**
*Global Keynote Speaker and Founder of 'Your Seat at the Table', Marketing Leader*

## About The Author: Rachel Pleasant

Currently serving as Chief Marketing Officer for a cybersecurity firm. Rachel Pleasant is an astute marketing leader who brings with her over two decades of marketing and leadership experience.

Rachel is also the founder of 'Your Seat at the Table', an initiative dedicated to providing women with the tools they need to ascend the corporate ladder and shatter glass ceilings.

This initiative includes a website, podcast, newsletter, and LinkedIn page that offers practical advice, resources, strategies, and inspiration that women can use as they advance along their own corporate journeys and strive to secure their own places at the corporate table.

Rachel is a seasoned speaker and delivers keynotes and workshops designed to empower women in the workforce. She shares valuable insights gained from her own journey to help women advance in their careers with greater speed and precision, leading them towards a more successful trajectory.

Based in California, Rachel enjoys spending time with her husband and three children as they explore the USA and experience the American culture as a family.

• • • • •

The day started like any other, with me loading my five-year-old twins and newborn daughter into the car to make the short drive to school. As the rising heat of the Florida sun kissed my skin and the soft breeze flowed through the window, a sense of contentment washed over me. I basked in the excited chatter of my twins and the gentle coos of my youngest as their sounds filled the vehicle.

As we slowly made our way up to the front of the kindergarten car line, I made eye contact with the twins, my son and daughter, in the rear-view mirror and said, as I said almost every morning, "Have a great day, guys, be good for the teacher, try your best, but most of all have fun and be kind!" I smiled, my gaze shifting between their bright faces.

What came next, however, caught me completely off guard. With innocence in his voice, my son turned to his sister and uttered a sentence that has stayed with me ever since.

"You don't need to do well because you're just going to have babies and stay at home with the kids."

The words hung in the air like the smell of a soiled diaper, a startling reminder to me of the beliefs that lie just beneath the surface, even in what I thought and hoped was a modern world.

My husband and I have always strived to raise our children with an intentional mindset around gender equality and self-determination, with the notion that you can achieve whatever you want to as long as you work hard. So, this casual remark utterly blindsided me. I could only surmise that this was primarily due to optics, given my work as a consultant had taken a temporary backseat due to the birth of our youngest and working from home while the children were at school or at night when they were sleeping.

After my initial shock and the briefest flash of disbelief that this had come out of my own son's mouth, I felt a fierce wave of determination come over me to set the record straight. (Really straight!)

Surprisingly, I responded rather calmly. "Buddy," I began, "your sister may not want to have children when she grows up. She might want to be a career woman, just like mommy. And when you grow up, if you get married and have children, your partner may want to work, and you might choose to stay home with the children. Or you may both decide not to have children at all. Both of you have many paths you can take in life, and that's why studying hard is important – so when you get to that point in life, you have options available to you."

I watched as my daughter's face lit up with a sparkle of confidence, her voice ringing out proudly, but maybe not as kindly as I would have liked. "Yeah!" At that moment, it felt like I had planted a tiny seed of empowerment and choice within their young minds, especially my daughter's.

There was a brief silence. Perhaps it was a moment of reflection in the minds of the two five-year-olds, or maybe merely a pondering on their upcoming recess adventures. Wherever their minds wandered, I hoped that, in some small way, our discussion had left a positive impression on them.

That evening, as I recounted the story to my husband, we made a pact to showcase actively to our children as they grow up, the incredible accomplishments of women, both around them and in the broader world. It became one of our key parenting commitments – to ensure that they grew up knowing that their potential was limitless, regardless of gender, and that they had the power to shape their own destinies.

We have found the 'Rebel Girls' book series to be an excellent starting point, with its inspiring tales of fearless women who have impacted the world in their unique ways. Additionally, we have made a conscious effort to seek out diverse books and movies that feature strong female characters and highlight the importance of gender equality. My youngest's favourite heroines are 'Captain America' and 'Wonder Woman'.

Recently, my husband and I listened to an audiobook by author Susanna De Vries, narrated by Jane Clifton, titled 'Great Australian Women: Inspiring Stories of Women Who Changed the Course of Australia.' In this book, Susanna De Vries spotlights the life stories of 18 courageous Australian women who defied gender bias, shattered the glass ceiling, and achieved awe-inspiring feats against all odds. We would play this in the car as we took family drives, and while the children wouldn't admit to listening, they would nevertheless occasionally mention something they had heard.

As a young girl, I was always fiercely independent and was determined to get ahead in life. My parents instilled the belief in my sister and I that we could be whatever we wanted to be if we were willing to work hard enough.

My dream career, from 2nd grade to 10th grade (Sophomore in the USA), was to become a police officer. I envisioned myself putting the bad guys away, like in the TV show 'CHIPS', an American crime drama from the '80s, dispensing justice and leaving the world a better place.

From the youngest age, I have always known that I wanted to make the world a better place, and at the time, I thought the way I would create that legacy was as a policewoman. Little did I know then that I would make my mark in a completely different way.

At the age of ten, my parents divorced, and we moved to a new area and a new school. We downsized from a house to a unit. Being a single parent was nowhere near as common at that time, with only three other families we knew of in our entire school hailing from divorced households. Seeing my mother struggle as a single mum fuelled my desire to do well at school and to get ahead even further.

However, this determination was put into overdrive after my mother met and married my stepfather, who initially appeared charismatic and caring; however, it became clear pretty quickly that he was an abusive man. Witnessing the effects of the emotional, physical and financial abuse he inflicted on my mother ignited a resolve to ensure I never had to rely on anyone for anything.

By the time we escaped my stepfather, I was in Grade 9 and fuelled with the desire to get ahead. As soon as I legally could, I started searching and landed a job at a small takeaway in our small country town. Years later, I discovered they hadn't really needed anyone, but because I was so persistent, they made a role especially for me.

From this first job at age 14, I worked every opportunity, afternoons to evenings, on late-night shopping days, weekends, and every day I could in the school holidays. I would often come home from the takeaway store smelling like doughnuts, fried Pluto Pups and Chico Rolls, for those who remember those classic Australian takeaway staples.

Even though this was casual work in the hours when I was not at school, I was super careful with my money, squirrelling away almost all my pay for several years. It turned out that over three years or so, I had saved up just over $8,000 from my $3-an-hour job. So when it came time to go to university, I had enough money to pay for my accommodation for the entire year, plus all my textbooks and incidentals. That was a proud moment that I will never forget.

After graduating from university, my first job was selling new cars for a large car dealership in regional NSW as a Sales and Marketing trainee. It was there that I got my first glimpse of the power of the patriarchy and a first-hand view of how one's gender can directly affect one's experience in the workforce and the potential trajectory of your career.

While working as an intern as a young female in a male-dominated industry, I often felt dismissed by my direct superiors, who assumed that I could not possibly understand the intricacies of cars and sales – it was 'a man's game!'

During my time in this position, I observed a sharp disparity in the treatment of males and females in the workplace. The male sales staff received mentorship and were presented with opportunities for advancement. On the other hand, the female sales staff were frequently assigned menial tasks such as fetching coffee, making the breakfast run to grab everyone bacon and egg rolls, or being asked to cover the reception desk when needed. This allocation of tasks directly affected the monthly earnings of these women in their commission-based roles. However, what was even more concerning was the long-term impact on their potential for future earnings due to limited access to training and mentorship opportunities.

While this situation may not be surprising to many, it was a harsh awakening as a newly graduated young woman filled with hope for an exciting career. The stark reality hit me as I observed how much gender can impact how one is viewed and treated in the workplace. This left a lasting sting. It felt incredibly unfair, and my young mind struggled to comprehend it.

This experience further fuelled my determination to challenge and dismantle these barriers wherever possible.

Not long after coming to this newfound realisation, I vividly recall heading over to my grandparent's house, with whom I shared an incredibly close bond. After sharing my experience, I was curious to ask my Nan about her experiences growing up and in the workforce. During our conversation, I asked whether she had encountered gender-based discrimination and if it had impacted her career and life trajectory. To my surprise, I discovered that back in her day, few women were encouraged to pursue education beyond marriage. If they did aspire to something beyond matrimony, secretarial school or nursing were the common options.

My Nan and Pop profoundly influenced my life and were always my biggest and loudest supporters, aside from my mother and father. In particular, as a woman, I admired Nan's frank demeanour, her no-nonsense attitude, her tendency to speak her mind, and her unwavering determination to forge ahead, no matter what challenges she encountered. As I pursued my business studies at university, I remained in awe of her professional journey, which she started by working in the deli department of a renowned grocery chain, eventually becoming their first-ever State Manager.

She worked hard, staking her claim in what I can only imagine was a challenging environment to achieve the remarkable success she did.

During our conversation, I posed a hypothetical question: If she could go back in time and pursue any career she desired, what would she choose? To my astonishment, she replied, "A brain surgeon." At first, I questioned the seriousness of her answer. Still, as we delved deeper into the topic, I realised she was genuinely serious. Then, it dawned on me how she would be captivated whenever an operation or medical procedure was shown on television. By contrast, I would, without fail, close my eyes and hum a tune or talk, trying to shield myself from the graphic footage. Blood, gory accidents, and medical procedures are not my cup of tea. But Nan would eagerly comment about the intricacies of the procedure, finding it utterly fascinating. Needless to say, she and Pop found my aversion to anything medical amusing. Oh, how I miss those two extraordinary individuals!

I do still think back to that conversation often and wonder how different her life may have been had she had the opportunity to pursue her passion for all things medical.

Escaping the car industry, I plunged into my marketing career, working for some of the largest tech companies from around the world. I found moving to Sydney and working with some of the brightest minds in tech was more than a breath of fresh air; it was a life changer.

During this time, I was fortunate to work under the guidance of some remarkable managers (both female and male) who have risen to very prominent leadership positions in Australian and global business.

In marketing, I often worked for women leaders. Their journeys and leadership styles always fascinated me, as did the reactions of other leaders towards them.

One of the most inspiring managers I've had was a phenomenal woman who demonstrated exceptional leadership qualities. Her ability to lead her team, navigate the corporate landscape, and build empires left a lasting impression on me. Her astuteness in bending the rules, adapting to situations, and navigating the corporate network was awe-inspiring. Moreover, she possessed the rare ability to communicate candidly while relating to individuals at all levels. Currently, she holds the esteemed position of General Manager for one of Australia's largest and most established organisations, where she continues to accomplish remarkable feats.

As I advanced in my career, I found it both fascinating and frustrating when I encountered a male leader or peer who believed their gender endowed them with inherent knowledge. However, this didn't deter me on my journey up the ladder. As I grew in my confidence and leadership abilities, I realised that my viewpoints, approaches and ideas were, in fact, not only equal but sometimes more robust than those of my male counterparts.

While I am grateful for the strong female role models who demonstrated how far women can go in their careers, upon reflection, it would have been wonderful to have had a platform or website dedicated to providing valuable leadership advice and guidance for women in navigating the complexities of the workforce. I believe that such a resource could have been an incredibly valuable tool for advancing not only my career but also that of my peers.

When I was in the trenches, I was unaware of the existence of career coaching, which was still in its infancy. Additionally, available business books primarily focused on cultivating a positive mindset rather than addressing specific skills required for women to navigate and advance their professional journeys.

It wasn't until a coaching session with a team member, when I was talking them through some self-promotion tactics in the workplace, that they mentioned, "You know, you should make this a guidebook. They don't teach this in school." This is when I had my "Aha!" moment. (Thanks for the term, Oprah.)

Throughout my 20+ year marketing career, I've been privileged to lead various teams, projects and individuals, including talented female professionals, always striving to share my knowledge with them to help them navigate and advance their careers. However, after this conversation, I realised that my guidance was only helping a select few, leaving so many without support.

Even today, accessible platforms offering information on corporate navigation and leadership development for women remain scarce or involve expensive memberships or subscriptions.

Recognising this need and in alignment with the commitment my husband and I made to demonstrate to our children the incredible capabilities of women and their ability to pursue any path they desire, I launched 'Your Seat at the Table.' This initiative comprises a website, newsletter, podcast, and LinkedIn page dedicated to empowering women in the workforce. It aims to provide them with valuable information, inspiring stories, practical advice, and effective strategies to help them achieve their potential and secure their positions at the corporate table.

Coming from my humble background, I felt it was important for women from all over the world, no matter their socio-economic background, to have access to a platform that could provide them with information and practical advice that is crucial for them to ascend the corporate ladder.

Even though I believed my legacy would be in law enforcement, helping women to succeed feels like my true calling, where I can still help make the world a better place – even if it is in a small way.

A significant incident that solidified my resolve to support women occurred during a dinner out with friends. One of our companions, a CEO, shared stories about his upbringing. He casually mentioned how his prominent businessman father would often engage in business discussions with him when he was growing up. They would exchange ideas, and the young CEO-to-be would consistently learn from his father's mentorship. This friend, who possesses exceptional networking skills, today follows in his father's footsteps, efficiently leveraging connections to foster collaborations in business.

While this revelation may not be groundbreaking, it profoundly highlighted to me the value of mentorship, role models, networking, and social connections.

As someone who came from a modest socio-economic background, I previously believed that sheer hard work was the sole path to advancement. However, this realisation forced me to acknowledge the advantages that these other elements bring to one's success.

After the dinner, I discussed this with my husband and contemplated how our lives and careers might have differed if we had benefited from similar support in our youth. The presence of someone who recognised our worth, possessed the experience to guide and nurture our abilities, and exposed us to valuable opportunities, networks, and connections could have significantly impacted our trajectory.

I lament that throughout history, systems in society have traditionally been built to help men succeed and get ahead in their careers. As women, we have not really had similar networks available to us. From a young age, boys have traditionally had access to groups such as Scouts and Boys Brigade, teaching them leadership skills and building social networks.

Although times are thankfully changing, I am proud to be part of a growing movement that supports and empowers women to advance and succeed in their careers.

Every woman deserves access to practical information, mentorship, role models, networking opportunities, and connections that can help elevate them in their careers.

This newfound but powerful insight has stayed with me ever since and continues to inspire me in my mission to help women in their career journeys.

According to the Workplace Gender Equality Agency's (WGEA) most recent report, 'Gender Equity Insights 2023', much work still needs to be done to achieve workplace equality. Some key findings from the report include:

- Women are consistently underrepresented among the top 20% of earners in most industry sectors.
- While the share of company boards chaired by women has increased by 2.3 percentage points to 16.7% over three years to 2022, we still have a long way to go to achieve equality.
- While the gender pay gap in Australia has fallen consistently over the past eight years to 22.8% in 2022, women in Australia still earn about 77% of men's earnings in 2022.

Despite the challenges and obstacles faced as a woman in the workforce, I am grateful for the inspiring female leaders who have paved the way and continue to inspire future generations. Their stories and achievements serve as a reminder that anything is possible with determination, resilience, and strong leadership skills.

As we continue on this journey for equality, I hope that by sharing our experiences and supporting each other, we can empower more women to break barriers and reach new heights in their careers.

Let us continue to uplift, amplify and fuel the voices of all women in leadership roles, creating a brighter future for the next generation and all future generations until we achieve equality.

Let's empower each other to chase our dreams and succeed in our careers.

Finally, 'Cheers' to all the incredible women out there, making their mark, breaking barriers, and shattering glass ceilings every day!

**References:**

BCEC | WGEA Gender Equity Insights 2023.
Sourced from *https://www.wgea.gov.au/publications/gender-equity-insights-series*

Chapter 6

# Brighter than the Sun: A Journey from Trials to Triumph in Leadership

**Angela Sedran**
*Global Keynote Speaker, Strategy and Leadership Consultant, Coach and Mentor*

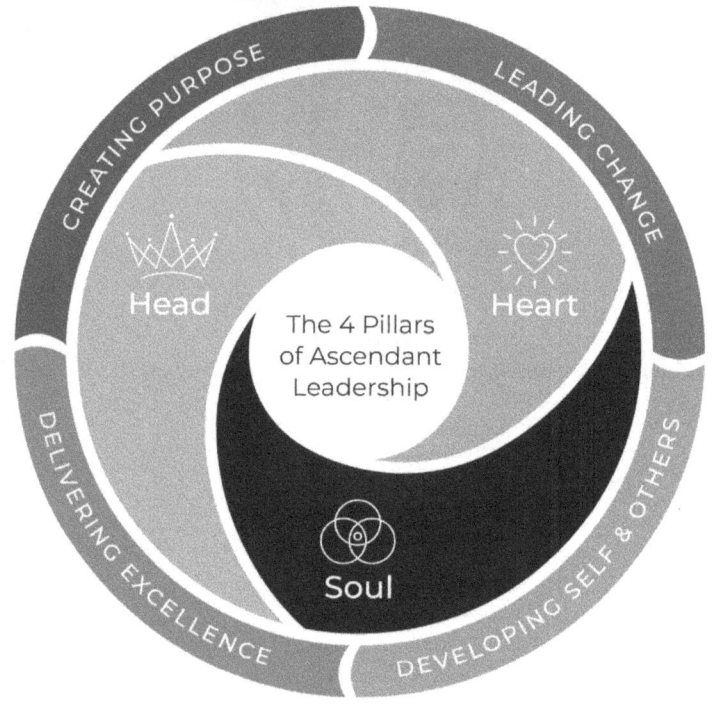

## About The Author: Angela Sedran

Angela Sedran, a dedicated mentor and consultant, guides dynamic, ambitious women through the intricacies of leadership and business strategy. With roots in both Italy and Germany, she brings a dynamic blend of expertise as a management consultant, leadership coach, and engaging public speaker. Her primary goal revolves around empowering women to step confidently into leadership roles. Angela's vision extends beyond herself; she aspires to lead a movement, aiming to support a million women in achieving financial freedom by 2030.

Angela's academic prowess shines through her Bachelor of Commerce and MBA from the Australian Graduate School of Management, underscoring her commitment to excellence. The Business Growth Accelerator, a finalist in the 2023 Business Xcellence Awards, stands as a testament to her relentless pursuit of quality and innovation.

Renowned as an industry leader, Angela embodies seasoned expertise as a Management Consultant and globally accredited Executive Coach, and is a member of the Australian Institute of Company Directors and the International Coaching Federation. A distinguished member of the Forbes Coaches Council, the Australian Institute of Company Directors, and an Executive Contributor to Brainz Magazine, Angela is a force to be reckoned with in the business realm.

Her unparalleled 15-year journey in strategic advisory has propelled businesses into the top echelons of revenues, marking her exceptional talent in scaling enterprises into multi-million-dollar successes. However, Angela's clients attest that her impact transcends financial success; it's about crafting authentic leaders destined for greatness.

Beyond her professional triumphs, Angela's vibrant life unfolds as a devoted single mother and a companion to her beloved Malshi, Mia. Her fluency in five languages and her daring spirit paint her as an globetrotter, adventure seeker, and advocate for life's richest experiences. Her adventures, from climbing glaciers to dancing the tango in Buenos Aires, are a testament to her zest for life and her determination to achieve the impossible.

• • • • •

If you'd have told me I would be approached by a publisher to write on the topic of Ascension Leadership prior to a sliding door moment I experienced in my early forties, I'd have thought you were crazy.

I say that because I was living on a knife's edge, struggling to hold my life together after going through a gut-wrenching divorce, as well as being scammed out of every cent I had, and left wearing a six-figure debt I had nothing to do with generating.

Yet here I am!

These days I get to coach wonderful women to rise above their limiting beliefs and step into their power to make the dent in the universe they've been put on this planet to make.

I find it fascinating to delve into the backgrounds that have shaped the women who come to me with so much potential, yet so little to show for it.

So, I figured you might like to know a little bit about my background as well. I'm not sharing this information with you to boast about the way I've turned my life around. I'm sharing it with you so that you can come away from reading this chapter thinking that if Angela can set herself up with a life where she wakes up every morning knowing she is making a difference in spite of the adversity life has thrown at her, then so can I.

I'm going to start my story from the time when I met my son's father at the ripe old age of 18. He was in his early thirties with an established career, and I fell madly in love with him. I gave birth to our son when I was 20 and I felt like my life was pretty wonderful.

I was living in a beautiful home with my beautiful family. And it was great while it lasted, but the bottom fell out of my world a few months after my son was born when two policemen knocked on the door with the news that my partner had been shot and killed. Whilst this type of horrific crime was a daily occurrence in South Africa, where I was born and raised, no one ever thinks something like this will happen to them - until it does.

My world fell apart in front of my eyes as I came to terms with being a young mother with very low earning potential raising a son on her own. I was only halfway through an accounting degree when I found myself solely responsible for myself and my little person. It wasn't easy, but I made it work with the money I earned through a part-time job in market research while finishing my degree and living with my parents.

Mandela's new government took over in 1994. Everyone was joyous and optimistic about the new rainbow nation South Africa had become. But the crime rate kept rising, and the currency continued to devalue, making it harder and harder for people to survive, both literally and figuratively. We were constantly living in fear of being kidnapped, raped or murdered - or all three. In fact, my biggest fear was being hijacked and having my car taken with my son still strapped in the back seat. This had happened to many others, and eventually it became clear to me that we had to leave South Africa because it was just too dangerous.

So in 1997, my parents, my nonna, my son and I, accompanied by our ten dogs, moved to Australia. This was an opportunity for which we will be forever grateful. However, shortly after becoming economic refugees in the country I still call home, I learned that resettling on the other side of the world under the circumstances we were in at the time was not for the faint-hearted. Among other things, the result of converting our money into Australian dollars was not nearly enough to secure anything like the kind of lifestyle we'd left behind.

Essentially, we were financial refugees starting over again in a new country, with no one but ourselves to rely on. Nevertheless, I was determined to build a good life for myself and my son. The only problem was that Australia was a very expensive place to live, and I couldn't afford to move out of my parents' place for the first few years we were there.

My son was also seriously falling behind the other kids he went to school with because it turned out that he was technically deaf owing to the multiple ear infections he was plagued with from a very young age. This caused the progressive loss of his hearing to the point where he could only sense sound through the bone rather than the eardrum, and, to compensate, he taught himself to lip-read. Life's curveballs can sometimes throw us off, but I've realised it's all about bouncing back. It's about sifting through those experiences, finding the little gems – the lessons, the memories, the growth – and cherishing them. Even when things don't go as planned, there's always something valuable we can take away.

Obviously, the learning and development he'd missed out on during that period couldn't be restored overnight. In fact, he actually needed years of expensive remedial teaching. This wasn't cheap, but I was determined to do whatever it took to give him the best opportunities I possibly could.

Determined to elevate our future, I embarked on an MBA journey. Gratefully, I was awarded a scholarship for my first year. The journey was intense, and I'm indebted to my parents for their support with my son during this time. Commitment isn't just about saying 'yes'; it's about facing every challenge head-on and finding ways to persevere. In a class where only 28% were women, I stood tall, proud to be among those breaking barriers. Whilst it did give me an income boost, it wasn't quite the onethat I had hoped for at the time because I graduated into a depressed post 9/11 market.

For the next 14 years I threw myself into my corporate career, focusing on earning as much as possible to give my baby boy all the help he needed. I was determined to do everything in my power to make sure he would achieve his dream of becoming an engineer. And he did. I feel like I'm the proudest mother ever because of the beautiful young man my son has become.

As hard as I tried, I was never completely happy in corporate life. Spending the day making money for huge corporations failed to make my soul sing (to say the least). I also hated the politics of corporate culture. There always seemed to be something disingenuous and unauthentic about it. That's why I can see in hindsight that being retrenched during the GFC was a blessing in disguise.

That said, the legacy of finding out I was being ousted still gives me nightmares to this day. I started two businesses in the year it took me to find another job. One involved making soy-based candles, and the other was an online women's sensuality boutique. One thing these businesses taught me is that we don't know what we don't know. And for my part, I didn't have a clue about how to raise funds to grow my businesses. My candles sold well, but it took a lot of work to make them, and they were difficult to transport because the jars they were housed in were glass. My online boutique also proved popular, but an e-store like that involves having stock on hand which ties up a lot of cash.

Essentially, I needed an equity partner and a business coach to grow, but I didn't know how to find either in 2007. So I found myself resorting to the 'safety' of the corporate world and a regular income as a result of listening to the little voice in my head that convinced me I wasn't good enough to be successful working for myself. I also suffered from paralysing anxiety around my fear of not making enough money.

In hindsight, I can see that I was partially right about not being good enough. I say that because unless I worked out how to overcome my money blocks, it was inevitable that I would fail outside at the 'trading time for money' scenario that salaried workers, like I used to be are locked into.

Looking back on it now, I can see that my life was going well for a period. I had a steady job as a management consultant and executive coach, and I married again in 2012. I finally felt secure because I had a dependable job and a man I loved who I was building a life with. It felt like we were a good team. My husband was trying to develop an idea he had into a new business, so I stepped up to be the full-time breadwinner. Admittedly my life was very busy, but I did what I did with love because that's what you do for your life partner.

We had each other's back - or so I thought!

A medical investigation in 2015 around the reason I'd lost my sense of taste lead to the discovery of a lesion on my brain. As if that wasn't bad enough, I found out that my husband was having an affair. The kicker was that he spent more money in three weeks on his "friend" than he spent on me during our entire relationship.

I remember confronting him. With utter disgust for me on his face and tears in his eyes, he said, "You are such a selfish bitch! You could be dying of a brain tumour. All I am doing is trying to find a replacement wife, and you are denying me that!" And that was that. I duly thanked him and immediately cut him out of my life. Saying that was the best thing he'd ever done for me.

The next year was really beautiful. I focussed on rebuilding my life, starting with putting a plan in place to pay off all the sexually-transmitted debt my husband had left me with. The plan involved opening a new limited-time zero interest credit card and rolling the balance over, using the money I saved on interest to pay off the debt.

And before too long, I was back in the black, not only in terms of my finances, but also in terms of my health because I had made a concerted effort to really look after myself. I was enjoying my independence and felt really empowered.

The only problem was that I got the shock of my life three days before Christmas 2015 when I logged into my bank account to check if I'd been paid. It was so lucky that I checked, because every single one of my credit cards was maxed out to the tune of nearly $100k.

The FBI, the Met and the Australian Federal Police all told me to give up, but I didn't – because I felt I had nothing left to lose. And in July 2016, I found a website that mentioned the name of the "company" involved in this scam. I'll never know why, but I shared my story, and within an hour, I received an anonymous email outlining who the perpetrator was. An Israeli by the name of Shir Gad-el. This was a common Israeli scam, not illegal in Israel but quickly becoming an embarrassment to the Israeli government. My source provided a screengrab of Gad-el's Facebook page and some background information. Gad-el had spent time in South America and spoke a bit of Spanish. The photo was of a fat, hairy, smug man lying on a pink pool flamingo floating on a pool. The last piece of information was an email address.

First, I contacted the Times of Israel, a reporter by the name of Simona Weinglass. Then I contacted my new friend, Shir Gad-el. I told him that I would be in Tel Aviv the following week to start civil proceedings against him and that I was talking to the Times. Also, if he didn't refund me immediately, I would set Interpol on him. I knew where he lived and that I had a detective watching him. "Don't believe me?", I told him, "Then how come I know you have a pool and pink pool flamingo, and that you speak Spanish?" He replied within 2 hours, and the refunds started flowing back in. It took a month of nagging to get them all back, but I got them. He told me that he had never been so depressed as when he met me. I assured him that the feeling was mutual. A friend of mine who worked in high-level security warned me off multiple times and told me that I had no idea who I was dealing with. These people could be organised crime. They had taken $100k off me and it apparently only cost $20k to put a contract on someone. Maybe I was stupid, but I didn't care. I was standing up for myself and that was that. In the end, I also insisted he give me the interest of 8 months of 22% of credit card debt back. And he did. Although, the Times of Israel article was ready to go, I did ask Simona not to publish because I thought that perhaps I had pushed my luck as far as it could go.

This all happened in August 2016. That is a month I will never forget. I say that because at the same time as I recouped my stolen funds, my divorce came through, and my employer retrenched a few staff, including me. I'll never forget what it felt like when the bullies I worked with met with me, and with some trepidation, gave me the news that my services weren't required anymore. I think they expected me to cry or something, but I burst out laughing instead. In fact, if there was a world speed record for someone packing up their desk and leaving a building, I would have won it that day for sure.

The upshot of what went on here is that I thought to myself - "to hell with it! I am going to work for the best boss in the world – me!" And I did. This time I went into business fortified by pure passion emanating from the realisation that what I care deeply about is helping women achieve financial freedom and independence. I figured that if I could help even one woman live a better life, mine would have been a life well spent.

By the time Covid shook our foundations and proved itself to be nothing if not a rapid catalyst for change, I was well and truly comfortable with change (which a lot of people are not). For me, the pandemic presented a great opportunity to morph my business into one that helps accelerate million dollar plus businesses in 90 days to greater profits, higher performance and more engaged teams with the right management systems and leadership.

I still do that, but my focus now is more on harnessing the untapped power within executive women to ensure they are not overlooked in the corporate world where they have so much to offer, especially when they master the competitive edge the Ascension Leadership approach provides them with.

So, let's take a look at what Ascension Leadership actually is.

**The Ascension Leadership Model**

I developed the unique approach to the Ascension Leadership model because in a world undergoing rapid change, the need for women in leadership roles has never been more pressing. The world needs more female leaders.

Meanwhile, traditional leadership models are increasingly falling short. I say that because they are lacking both emotional intelligence and the elements needed to cultivate trust. Whereas Ascension Leadership goes beyond focusing only on achieving success because it also promotes personal growth, self-awareness, and positive transformation.

In other words, Ascension Leadership is a holistic approach that is based on the idea of prioritising personal and collective growth over things like power, control, and exclusively focusing on the bottom line. Paradoxically, bottom line results improve dramatically within organisations where Ascension Leadership is practiced.

Before I go into the specifics of my own approach, I want to fill you in on the key principles that underpin Ascension Leadership.
They are:

1. Self-awareness: AAscension-focussed leaders prioritise self-awareness as the foundation of their leadership journey. They continually strive to understand their strengths, weaknesses, values, and motivations. This self-awareness allows them to make conscious choices and align their actions with their values.
2. Empathy and compassion: Ascension leaders consistently cultivate empathy and compassion, not just for their team members, but for all of their stakeholders. They understand that the wellbeing of individuals and the community is essential for sustainable success.
3. Collaboration and inclusivity: Ascension leaders encourage collaboration and inclusivity, valuing diverse perspectives and ideas. Leaders using this model seek to build a culture of trust and openness where everyone's contributions are valued.
4. Growth mindset: Ascension leaders embrace a growth mindset, believing that they can learn and grow throughout their lives. They encourage their team members to adopt a similar attitude, promoting continuous learning and improvement within the organisations they run.
5. Purpose-driven leadership: Ascension leaders are driven by a higher purpose that goes well beyond the imperative of profit. They aim to make a positive impact on society, aligning their organisations' missions with values that serve the greater good.

## The Benefits of Ascension Leadership

1. Personal growth and fulfillment: Ascension leaders experience personal growth as they become more self-aware, compassionate, and purpose driven. This growth leads to a deep sense of fulfillment and meaning in their life.
2. Enhanced team performance: Ascension leaders create a supportive and inclusive work environment where team members feel valued and motivated. This, in turn, boosts morale and productivity.

3. Long-term success: Ascension Leadership promotes sustainability by focusing on holistic growth and ethical decision-making. Organisations led by Ascension leaders are more likely to thrive in the long run.
4. Innovation and adaptability: The culture of continuous learning and collaboration fostered by Ascension Leadership encourages innovation and adaptability. Where this is the case, teams are more open to experimenting with new ideas and responding to change positively.
5. Positive impact on society: Ascension leaders make a positive impact not only within their organisations, but also in the broader community. Their purpose-driven approach leads to socially responsible practices and initiatives.

Several prominent leaders exemplify the principles of Ascension Leadership. One notable figure is Patagonia's founder, Yvon Chouinard, who built a company with a strong commitment to environmental sustainability and social responsibility. Another example is Oprah Winfrey, whose leadership style is marked by empathy, compassion, and a desire to empower others. Through her media empire and philanthropic efforts, she has made a significant impact on individuals and society as a whole.

**My Approach**

I go deep when I work with clients to fast track their leadership potential. I do that by applying my 4 Pillars of Ascendant Leadership. These cover the heart, the head, the soul, and the spheres of influence.

The work we do on the heart fortifies our ability to forge genuine emotional connections. Meanwhile the work we do on the head governs our intellectual faculties and strategic thinking, while the soul work we do creates character and an aura that emanates trustworthiness and integrity. Meanwhile the spheres of influence component of the 4 Pillars concentrates on the external practices we leverage to influence our outcomes. Essentially, it acts as the catalyst that transforms our internal qualities into tangible actions and results.

Within this paradigm, the head, heart and soul can be seen as internal holistic elements that guide and inform a leader's approach in general and their mindset in particular. In other words, these are the foundational elements that shape the way a leader thinks, feels, and establishes trust.

On the other hand, the spheres of influence are essentially the external, visible manifestations of leadership. Another way of looking at this is to think of the trifecta of the head, heart, and soul as the inner core attributes that provide the fire of external leadership that results in the spheres of influence we are able to create.

The point I'm making here is that just as fire requires the right balance of elements to burn brightly and effectively, so too a leader requires a balanced set of attributes to catalyse the expertise and energy within themselves and the organisations they oversee.

This kind of symbiotic relationship between the internal and external elements provides a full spectrum view of what it takes to be a fully effective leader.

**Conclusion**

Ascension Leadership offers a transformative approach to leadership that goes beyond traditional models. By prioritising personal growth, empathy, collaboration, and purpose driven endeavours, Ascension leaders create environments where individuals and organisations can flourish.

In an ever-changing world, this style of leadership has the potential to inspire positive change and contribute to a more compassionate and sustainable future for all.

Whether you are a corporate leader or business owner looking to evolve your approach and take your results to a whole other level, or an aspiring leader hungry to make a difference, the principles of Ascension Leadership can help unlock your full potential and make a lasting impact on the world.

angelasedran.com

linkedin.com/in/angelasedran

@yourbadassbusinesscoach
@theladybossbusinesscoach

Connect with me

Chapter 7

# Your Health is your Wealth

**Kama Atcheson**
*Global Keynote Speaker, Elite Woman in Finance (MPA Magazine, 2022)*

## About The Author: Kama Atcheson

Kama Atcheson stands as an illustrious figure in the Australian finance industry, boasting a formidable 24-year legacy that defies convention. Her journey is a testament to enduring excellence, underscored by her dedication to empowering others and the broader community.

Kama's focus is her mission to demystify the complexities of personal, commercial and business finance. She is passionate about fostering financial literacy.

Kama engages through podcasts, blogs, social media, webinars, and speaking engagements. She holds numerous awards and nominations and her involvement as a judge for the MFAA Excellence Awards further attests to her commitment to enhancing the finance sector.

Kama's portfolio includes arranging finance for some of the most prestigious developments in Australia and her dedication to education mirrors her active involvement with industry associations.

Her role as a judge for the MFAA Excellence Awards demonstrates the high esteem in which she is held within the industry, and solidifies her position as an inspirational force in shaping the finance sector. Her insights and quotations in renowned publications such as The Adviser and MPA Magazine further highlight Kama's influence.

In a remarkable milestone, she was recognized as one of the Elite Women in Finance for 2022 by MPA Magazine, standing alongside an exceptional cohort of women from around the world. This recognition reinforced her enduring impact and dedication to fostering diversity and empowerment within the finance industry.

Kama Atcheson's journey is a tapestry of sustained excellence, innovation, and empowerment. Her thought leadership transcends conventional boundaries, inspiring positive change for industry professionals, clients, and the broader community. Kama is more than a finance expert; she is a dynamic force dedicated to reshaping the finance landscape with unwavering commitment to the betterment of all.

• • • • •

I invite you to embark on a journey through my life – a journey that's influenced by my early life experiences, a career in finance, and a life-altering revelation that forever changed my perspective. My name is Kama Atcheson, and this is a tale of how your wealth is intricately tied to your health.

I was born in Coffs Harbour, a coastal gem known as "banana town." Imagine the aroma of bananas filling the air, as the rhythm of life was synchronized with the waves of the ocean. This idyllic setting provided me with a love for a lifestyle that harmonized with the beach and nature.

As a young girl, I was fortunate to enjoy opportunities to travel to Sydney and other vibrant cities around the world, thanks to my mother's pioneering role in the fashion and style industry. You see, I grew up in a family of entrepreneurs. Both my mum and dad, along with our extended family, were immersed in various small businesses. These early years offered me insights into the challenges and rewards of small business ownership. That's where I began my journey, a quiet little place that seemed a world away from the finance industry, where I'd eventually make my mark.

As I reached high school, a new dimension of life unfolded. I was accepted into a performing arts school, an environment brimming with artistic and creative souls. Dance, drama and singing became a significant part of my life. Yet, beyond the dance floor, another passion cultivated during my upbringing on the farm thrived within me – my love for animals. Horses, in particular, captured my heart.

Outside of dancing, I spent a significant part of my youth riding. I devoted approximately eight hours each week to dance classes, and whenever I could, I embarked on horse riding adventures. I cherished the sense of freedom and connection with nature that came from riding. In fact, my first venture into financial independence was the purchase of a car so that I could acquire a horse, a decision that marked the beginning of my independence.

I had been riding for years, dedicating my weekends to this passion. But riding came with its risks. I encountered several accidents, resulting in broken bones and visits to the hospital for X-rays and casts from the age of six. The most vivid memory is of a proud day when, at 16, I bought my very own horse with the money I had saved from working. What followed was the addition of many more horses, each serving different purposes in equestrian activities, from showing to sporting and eventing. My journey with horses was also truly cherished by my BFF Marija, and we enjoyed many rides and adventures together. My family, it seems, couldn't escape the allure of horses either. As a result of my passion, we transitioned into what one might affectionately call a "horse family". We acquired property to accommodate this new lifestyle.

My fondness for horses was unwavering, even in the face of daunting accidents. The first fracture occurred when I was just a first-grader, a result of bareback riding, then another in my first year of high school that left my left collarbone shattered into three pieces. That was a harrowing experience, but it didn't break my spirit or dim my love of riding.

In my early twenties, I experienced what remains the scariest moment of my life. A horse-riding adventure took a perilous turn. I vividly remember an intense crash – I flew through the air and plunged headfirst into the ground, my feet in their RM William boots flipping up over my head, kicking me in the back of my skull before I smashed into a bed of unforgiving rocks. I lay winded on the side of a steep, bushy bank, afraid to move, unsure if my legs were paralysed. The loud, cracking noise that resonated in the air following my fall had come from my back. The thought that dominated my mind as I lay there, frozen with fear, was clear and haunting – "If I am a paraplegic or quadriplegic, I don't want to live." **This fear of losing the use of my legs, of being confined to a wheelchair, ran deep within me, a terror that would resurface later in life.** This deep-seated fear would later resonate in my work life and experiences, serving as a constant reminder of the connection between well-being and prosperity.

That haunting memory returned when my mom succumbed to cancer just before I gave birth. The realm of childbirth, particularly the anticipated agony and the procedures that promised painlessness, made me anxious. Epidurals and caesareans, the standard choices, especially within the private system, didn't resonate with me. The thought of giving birth without feeling my legs was scarier to me than the idea of enduring the pain of childbirth itself. This led to a crucial decision to opt for a natural birth.

My choice was met with mixed reactions, and I felt somewhat isolated in my decision. To face this apprehension, I reached out to two individuals who would be my pillars of strength: my best friend, Carly, and a lady named Juju Sundin. Carly's role in my life extended beyond friendship; she is my son's godmother, and her presence during my birthing experience was the embodiment of support and courage. Juju Sundin, an expert in childbirth, became my guide in pain management. I discovered Juju's book, "Birth Skills," which featured Sarah Murdoch, and reaching out to Juju for support and asking her to be my midwife brought a new dimension to my journey, as my connection with her set me on a path to conquering this fear. It was a journey into the unknown, but having people like Carly and Juju by my side made it bearable. This decision ultimately showcased the strength that resides within us when we face our deepest fears.

Amid these pivotal events and defining events, one undeniable fact emerged: my family played a significant role in shaping my outlook on life. My mother, in particular, was a visionary in Australia. She co-founded a pioneering business in the early '80s, Colour Magic, alongside Gerry Harvey's ex-wife Lyn. This business focused on analysing individual colours, features, and shapes, ultimately helping people elevate their personal style and dress for success. My mother's consultations extended to numerous professionals and A-list celebrities, and I fondly recall the high-spirited parties that enlivened our home during this time.

My mother eventually sold this business and ventured into the world of fashion. Our house was transformed into a hub of creativity, with racks of clothes, rolls of fabrics, and design patterns scattered throughout. It became a regular destination for models and fashion enthusiasts. My mother's work seeped into my daily life, and from the age of five, I was often clacking around the house in her high heels, revelling in the world of fashion and style.

Meanwhile, my father operated a successful construction and development business. His team of project managers managed various projects, and I played an active role as a teenager, assisting with administrative tasks and payroll. My favourite duty was calculating expenses each week to ensure everything aligned for accounting purposes, a process that relied heavily on manual calculations due to the absence of modern accounting software.

Beyond their professional endeavours, my parents frequently hosted charity events and extended their help to individuals seeking success in the world of business. As a child, I often found myself preparing coffee and tea for my parents' client meetings. In many ways, this early exposure to a dynamic and influential network fostered my innate ability to connect with others and engage in meaningful conversations.

These are the building blocks of my early life, a period that laid the foundation for what was to come. But how did I transition from horses and fear to the world of finance? The answer lies in a simple conversation with my dad that changed the course of my life.

It was a sunny Sunday afternoon, and my dad shared his experience with obtaining development finance. The topic piqued my curiosity, and I decided to explore it further. Rather than submitting job applications, I took a more unconventional route – I created a job for myself. This was the year 1999, a time when finance brokers were a rare breed, and the industry was largely male dominated.

The question you might be pondering is, "How did I secure a job in such an environment?" The answer, while simple, holds a powerful lesson. I asked questions. I inquired about the industry, its needs, and where they sourced their business. Armed with this knowledge, I had a job to start the next day. Approaching real estate agents and establishing partnerships, aiding them in distributing their brochures at open houses, and providing potential clients with information about mortgage options.

Every Monday morning, I embarked on a ritual: I called everyone who had attended the open houses, offering them opportunities to explore their mortgage options and potentially secure a better deal. It was a mutually beneficial arrangement. For the real estate agents, it meant having serious, finance-approved clients. For me, it was a glimpse into how the world of real estate worked in Sydney's élite suburbs. This experience ignited my understanding of the value finance brokers bring to clients.

It wasn't long before I was writing a substantial number of transactions, a feat that was especially noteworthy given my age and the male-dominated environment I worked. The concept of the revolving line of credit became immensely popular, a financial product in high demand among my clients which epitomized the era. My journey evolved rapidly as I began working with high-profile real estate principals in Sydney's most exclusive suburbs. These principals also worked closely with developers in obtaining presales and linked me in with securing finance, and I found myself on the cutting edge of brokering complex deals. This experience illuminated the vital role that finance brokers play in helping clients navigate the intricate world of finance.

I was invited to lunches and dinners by banks and financial institutions, all eager to secure more business. One of the financial institutions I was sending business to recognized my potential and offered me a position as a Business Development Manager. My adventurous spirit led me to accept this opportunity, marking a significant change in my career direction. I began to understand the intricate world of risk and gained the ability to approve loans. This role enabled me to explore various areas, from credit to sales. This was a pivotal step in my journey. I later transitioned to roles where I trained staff on systems and processes, eventually moving into distribution.

My career trajectory allowed me to work with numerous financial institutions, ranging from major banks to specialist and challenger lending institutions. I stood at the forefront, working alongside finance brokers, equipping them with the tools and knowledge to better serve their clients. Given my background in credit and risk, I often found myself dealing with complicated transactions that fell outside the established policies. Today, my expertise and experience has made me a sought-after resource among finance professionals and clients, particularly when they encounter transactions that fall outside conventional lending parameters. My background in credit allowed me to offer valuable insights and guidance, a role I embraced wholeheartedly.

Over the years, I've been privileged to assist countless clients in obtaining the best financial advice and options. Yet, there's more to my journey than just a successful career in finance. Beyond the numbers and transactions, my mission lies in helping people transform financial chaos into clarity.

I've had the opportunity to witness the transformative power of effective financial advice. I worked closely with several finance brokers, accountants, and their clients, observing the positive impact of collaborative efforts. This journey unveiled the critical importance of having the right advisors in one's corner, whether it be accountants, financial advisors, bookkeepers, business consultants, or insurance and finance brokers. The recognition of the profound importance of having the right advice and the right people by your side cannot be overstated. Understanding who to work with and who to avoid can be life-changing, the difference between success and failure. It's a testament to the age-old saying: "It's not just what you know, it's who you know."

Many individuals have encountered financial challenges due to inadequate or incorrect advice. A dear friend who was at the pinnacle of her career, the chief revenue officer of a global marketing firm, serves as an example. She was on the cusp of starting a new job at another global company, only to fall ill unexpectedly and thus unable to take up her new role. With mortgage payments, private school fees and expensive overseas vacations, her world was turned upside down. Despite having financial safety nets in place, such as income protection, she faced an unexpected roadblock. Her policy didn't cover her since she was technically unemployed when she fell ill. The repercussions of this situation significantly affected her family's lifestyle and were a stark reminder of the importance of sound financial advice. Such stories are unfortunately far too common.

Let me share with you a deeply recent personal story, one that shook the very foundation of my beliefs. It's a tale of revelation and transformation, all rooted in the fundamental truth that "Your Wealth Is Your Health." In the midst of this eventful year, my personal journey of being a single working mum took an unexpected turn. Life, it seemed, had a way of teaching me its most valuable lessons.

The transformation began when I was hit by an autoimmune disease. The pain was so excruciating that I found myself bedridden, unable to move and **feeling like a shattered china doll**. Even the thought of turning over in bed seemed unbearable. It was like all my bones were broken. What was supposed to be a restful night turned into a nightmare. When I finally sought medical help, the doctor was taken aback by the severity of my symptoms. She remarked, "Why haven't you gone to the hospital already? You've had broken bones, you've given birth; you know what pain is." This was a pivotal moment; it signalled the gravity of my condition.

The journey following my diagnosis was, in a way, isolating. The pain, no matter how positive you try to remain, can wear you down. Fatigue coupled with sleeplessness due to steroids and an array of medications made it a physically and mentally exhausting ordeal. At one point, I broke out in a terrible rash that felt like being attacked by a million mosquitoes. My body was covered in red bumps and welts, so severe that I assumed I actually had a bad case of chickenpox. I was in relentless agony. It was as if my body was rebelling against me. Even in the midst of all this, I questioned whether it was all in my head.

In search of answers and support, I found online groups of people who shared my condition. It was a revelation; I wasn't alone, and my suffering was indeed real. I also recognized how fortunate I was compared to others. This experience was an obvious reminder that life could take unexpected turns, and our health is a treasure we often overlook until it's threatened.

This journey profoundly affected my self-perception. It prompted me to reevaluate what truly mattered in life. My career, a source of immense passion and satisfaction, shifted from being merely a profession to a calling. The profound realization hit me like a ton of bricks. I'm not just a professional; I'm on a vital mission to increase financial awareness and empower individuals to transform their financial well-being.

Financial wellness is a holistic and multidimensional concept that refers to an individual's overall financial health and well-being. It covers budgeting and planning, savings & rainy day funds, debt management, investing and wealth building, estate planning, and insurance & risk management. Being financially aware includes understanding the distinction between good and bad debt, discovering tools, products, and support that can alleviate cash flow issues and knowing how your credit rating can affect much more than just your financial life. The world of finance is vast, and even seasoned professionals often remain unaware of the multitude of options available.

Financial wellness embodies many elements, creating a comprehensive portrait of one's financial health and prosperity. It paints a picture that includes the art of budgeting and strategic planning, the comforting presence of savings and rainy-day funds, the delicate dance of debt management, the thrill of investing and wealth accumulation, the legacy we leave with estate planning, and the safety net of insurance and risk management. In this ever-evolving financial landscape, true financial well-being comes from recognizing the contrast between beneficial and detrimental debt, unearthing the array of tools, products, and expert support that can breathe life into cash flow concerns, and comprehending how to manage your credit rating and how it can impact you. The financial realm is a vast universe, and even seasoned professionals may find themselves navigating its intricacies without fully realizing the multitude of pathways. I aim to provide individuals with the networks and resources they need to achieve their financial goals, reduce financial stress, and improve their overall quality of life.

Having the right advice and the right people by your side can make all the difference. The significance of having the right accountant, financial advisor, bookkeeper, business consultant, insurance, and finance broker cannot be overstated. Often, it's a matter of having the right people in your corner – or working against you.

Through all these experiences, one thing became profoundly evident to me: the importance of approaching life with gratitude and a positive outlook. A happy heart, as they say, is a magnet for miracles. Even in the middle of my own health challenges, I was surrounded by a network of people who provided unwavering support.

It is from this vantage point—a life rich in experiences and personal trials—that I aim to foster a deeper understanding of financial wellness. Our physical and mental well-being are the foundations upon which we build our lives and our legacy.

As I move toward remission, I look forward to sharing my experiences and knowledge. My mission is to help more individuals navigate the path to financial prosperity. This journey involves connecting people and aiding them in making informed choices. It's about providing real solutions that can help them lead a life of financial well-being. My mission is to help more individuals transform financial chaos into clarity.

The realization that "Your Wealth Is Your Health" has become my guiding principle. Beyond the numbers and the transactions, I've come to believe that well-being is the bedrock upon which we build our dreams, our careers, and our lives.

The etymology of the word "wealth" itself underscores this connection, as it traces its roots to "weal," meaning well-being, and "health." My journey, shaped by early life lessons, a dynamic career in finance, and a life-altering health revelation, is a testament to this profound truth. I invite you to reflect on your own life, to appreciate the wealth that comes from good health, and to recognize that the pursuit of financial well-being should not be separate from the pursuit of overall well-being.

I encourage you to reflect on your own journey and the connections between your wealth and well-being. Remember that wealth is not just measured in dollars and cents, but in the richness of well-being that allows us to fully savour and appreciate all that life has to offer. I firmly believe that understanding the intricate relationship between wealth and health is not just my mission but a universal pursuit.

My life's purpose is now clear: to empower individuals, to transform financial chaos into clarity, and to remind the world that while financial success is a worthy pursuit, it should never come at the expense of health. Your health is your greatest wealth, and it's my mission to help you nurture and protect it on your journey to a prosperous life. Connect with me on LinkedIn, and let's embark on this transformative journey together.

This is not just the end of a chapter; it's the beginning of a purposeful life.

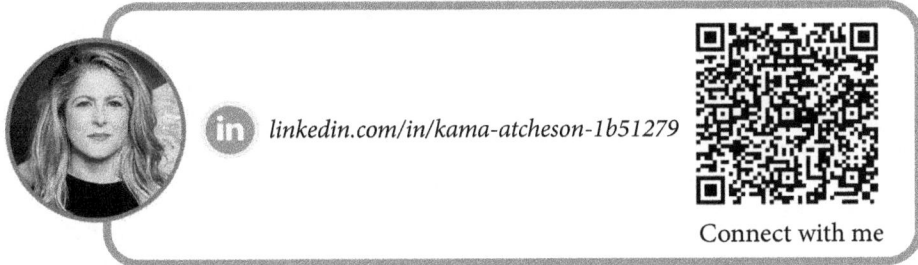

linkedin.com/in/kama-atcheson-1b51279

Connect with me

Chapter 8

# Proud to be Loud

**Pinky McKay**
*Global Keynote TEDx Speaker, International Board-Certified Lactation Consultant (IBCLC), Best-selling Author, Podcast Host*

## About The Author: Pinky McKay

Pinky McKay is one of Australia's most respected and recognised breastfeeding and early parenting experts. She is an International Board-Certified Lactation Consultant (IBCLC), a best-selling author with four titles published by Penguin Random House, TEDx speaker, podcast host (Tits Up) and an award-winning business woman.

After visiting many exhausted and nutritionally depleted new mothers struggling with their breast milk supply, Pinky created Australia's first range of lactogenic foods (boobiefoods.com.au). She also offers a Business Bootcamp for lactation professionals.

As a health professional, a mum of five (with eighteen years between the oldest and youngest), and a grandmother, Pinky has a unique perspective: she combines empathy for new parents and the pressures they face with education and guidance that is often presented with an irreverent sense of humour. She is both gentle and strong – standing firm as an advocate for breastfeeding, infants' needs and evidence-based information but simultaneously acknowledging that parents are the experts on their own child, and they need to be supported with kindness, inclusion, and acceptance of where they are right now.

Specialising in gentle, evidence-based parenting styles that honour mothers' natural instincts to respond to their babies, Pinky's books include 'Sleeping Like a Baby', 'Parenting by Heart', '100 Ways to Calm the Crying' and 'Toddler Tactics' (Penguin Random House).

Pinky's 'get real', no-nonsense approach, along with a blend of humour, sharp wit and wisdom, make her an expert source for national publications and major network TV.

• • • • •

**B**e quiet. Don't talk. Don't shout. Tone it down.
Just like the old phrase, 'children should be seen and not heard', the cultural messages for girls and women were strong. "Proper ladies aren't loud."

I defied the gentle voices of the women before me who 'knew their place' or at least were careful enough to rebel quietly, as well as the leather strap of my mother who did her best to 'tame' me. I was loud, impulsive and a director of mischief among the boys who lived nearest in our small New Zealand village.

On one hand, I was kicked out of classrooms, on the other, I was the kid chosen to speak up. At 12, I was the Master of Ceremonies at the district ANZAC service which was held at our little country school, introducing the dignitaries and veterans, including a very respected Victoria Cross serviceman.

Despite spending almost as much time outside the classroom for disrupting classes as I did attending lessons, I excelled academically. I was 'up there' with the brainy boys who were planning careers in law and medicine. I told my mother I wanted to study medicine. Her response was clear: "You are not wasting your father's hard-earned money on university. You're a GIRL! You'll get married and have babies."

My father did indeed work hard, as a truck driver. He had left school at ten years old and was possibly dyslexic; he could barely read or write but he was physically strong with an amazing work ethic and drive to support our family. My mother had undiagnosed and untreated bipolar disorder and between running my father's business when she was well, she spent months at a time in hospital when things went 'tits up'.

By the time I was 12, I was answering the phone and doing my father's accounts when Mum was in hospital. After school, each evening I would write down what jobs he had done, what loads he had carted that day, in the big black diary. Then on weekends, I would write up the accounts to be posted to his customers so we would have an income to support us.

Since I'd been told I would 'just' get married and have babies I couldn't really see the point in being a 'good girl' at school, nevertheless, I still blitzed exams. My mother was called up and asked to go to a meeting with my teachers. She told them, "I am not coming to any meetings; I've had a gut-full of her, too. You can do what you like with her!"

One day, Mum packed me up and drove me to the hospital in the next big town for an interview to train as a nurse. I didn't know any better, so was perfectly happy to leave home at sweet sixteen. After all, I wasn't going to university anyway. I wouldn't have known how to get into one, let alone how to survive in a big city.

During my first year as a nurse, my voice got me voted president of the student nurses association (I wasn't even aware I had been nominated!). I had been daring enough to take my breakfast to Matron's office and put my cold, rubbery eggs on her desk one morning. In those days, we practically kissed our senior staff's feet, we spoke when spoken to (quietly of course) and Matron and her deputy were treated with awe and fear. But I hadn't seen the point in bitching among ourselves. That wouldn't change anything. And, yes, Matron came down to the kitchen and sorted out the horrible staff food offerings.

Moral of the story – speak up, leaders aren't mind readers.

My mother hadn't completely given up on trying to make a lady of me and for my birthday she gifted me a deportment course with a former Miss New Zealand. A beautiful, elegant woman who taught us all sorts of lady-like skills – I can only remember practising walking down stairs with my head up, eyes front and descending smoothly without looking at my feet. After the classes had finished, I was asked if I'd like to do modelling. I was a tall, skinny girl so probably would have displayed the clothes pretty well, but I made my own clothes and had never owned a 'store-bought' dress.

"What?" I chortled. "Walking up and down in high heels with people staring at me? No bloody way!"

Instead, I continued emptying bedpans and taking care of sick people, occasionally getting into trouble for making too much noise – when a hard-of-hearing old bugger insists he wants you to put his penis into the urinal because he has 'double vision', of course you won't take his crap. I told him nice and loudly, "Look carefully and you will see two willies and two bottles, put one in each and pee."

Years later when I took one of my children to a psychology assessment for his dyslexia, the psychologist insisted on assessing me too and declared, "The mother has ADHD." That was 20 years ago, before it was 'acceptable' to be neurodivergent.

Although this may explain some of my 'spiritedness', having a label hasn't defined me. I am not medicated, and although my impulse to speak up without a filter isn't everybody's cup of tea, what other people think of me isn't my business. I do my best to be kind and respectful, but I won't ever be quiet if I see injustice or harm being done.

Fast forward, I travelled to Australia, met my husband and had the first of our five babies.

There was a paucity of information about baby care. There were a small number of books written by men in white coats, who most likely had 'good wives' bringing up their own babies, and a medical system that influenced women into believing that the (mostly male) doctors knew more about their bodies than generations of innate, intuitive female wisdom. Articles in women's magazines explained how many baby singlets, nappies and outfits we would need, along with knitting patterns for sweet little baby clothes.

I didn't know what I didn't know, and I was blissfully unaware of the challenges of being a newborn's mother.

At just a few days old, our baby developed an infection and was taken to Neonatal Intensive Care. I could barely express a teaspoon of precious liquid gold, but this didn't seem to matter to the hospital staff, because my baby was being fed formula in the nursery. Somehow, I trusted that when I got my baby back from NICU, my milk would come back.

One beautiful midwife took me under her wing and handed me a copy of a small blue book, 'The Womanly Art of Breastfeeding' a manual published by La Leche League, a breastfeeding support organisation started in the United States, that has grown internationally. When my baby was finally back with me, this wonderful woman 'let' me 'feed on demand' when the expectation was strict four-hourly feeding routines.

Despite modern babies having the same needs for nurturing as Stone Age infants, fads and fashions of baby care have kept on changing, with conflicting advice from 'experts' even in the same era. Is it any wonder that new mothers are confused?

I was confused too, as all the women around me seemed to have THEIR babies in a routine. Some were so organised they bathed their babies daily before the 6 am feed! I wasn't going anywhere that early, so I simply tucked my baby into bed beside me and latched him onto my breast. We dozed together.

I didn't watch the clock because I didn't see a need to count feeds any more than I needed to count kisses and cuddles.

By three months, I didn't know anyone else who was breastfeeding; all the local mums had weaned. It's really no surprise, because apart from 'wanting their bodies back' and added pressure to 'take care of your husband', a whole generation of women were conned into believing they had 'lost their milk.'

Rigid feeding routines didn't match babies' needs or mothers' individual milk storage capacities. Growth spurts and appetite increases were unheard of, and night feeds were dropped by six weeks, so of course this impacted milk supply. Unscrupulous formula manufacturers were advertising the benefits of the bottle for self-doubting mothers who were, understandably, terrified of starving their babies.

Sadly, as fads of baby care have come and gone and been repeated with various tweaks, mothers are still facing pressures around 'doing it right' and the division has grown between mothers choosing differing parenting styles.

When my fourth baby was a toddler, I was home-schooling my older kids. I had taken them out of school after a clash with teachers: one kid didn't 'conform'. "But does he cooperate?" I asked. "Yes, but he MUST conform!" I was told. After some discussion I told his teacher, "Hitler would've had a more difficult time if people hadn't simply conformed. We clearly have very different values around children's needs, so I don't know why I am giving my child to you for more hours of the day than he spends with me." I removed him from school, and he thrived. My other son was home with a broken arm that had happened at school as he'd fallen off play equipment. When I went to collect some work for him, I watched his classroom teacher call another child 'stupid' in front of the class. I didn't send him back either.

My mantra for doing anything with infants and children is: Is it safe? Is it respectful? Does it feel right? It felt right to speak up for my children, not as precious and delicate flowers but as people – children are people, too.

While my kids were learning at home and in the community, I found what I thought would be a fabulous creative activity for them. It was an entry assignment for 'Copy School', an advertising course. Although I didn't have a clue what a copywriter did, I sent my entry in.

This was the start of my writing career.

With over 2,000 entries, ten people were selected for this elite course, and I was among them. We went around Melbourne's top ad agencies learning from award-winning creative directors, with weekend workshops in a lovely country retreat. This was the late eighties – ad men drove Porsches and wore leather jackets and baggy pants. I took my breastfeeding two-year-old with me to weekend workshops, which was more shocking to everyone than their expensive booze was to me.

Here, my fearless voice was an advantage. We created ad campaigns for clients who had shared a brief on Friday night for us to work on over the weekend and present on Sunday afternoon. I presented print, radio and TV ads and won the Saturday night talent quests with comedy routines – I can't even clap in time let along sing in tune – all with my two-year-old in tow!

Although I was offered work in agencies when our year-long course finished, this wouldn't work with the kids (I didn't have family backup and my husband travelled for work) so I got a one-day-a-week job writing ads and started my own freelance business.

I learned some great lessons in Business 101:

I learned how to ask for money – this was a big lesson when mothering was so devalued (and still is): I told one client who didn't pay on time, I would be bringing my kids with Vegemite sandwiches and yoghurt to run loose in his shop until he paid me!

I learned how to handle what would now be classed as sexual harassment – the '#metoo' movement was still years away. One client who fancied me, started calling into my home without an appointment and one afternoon invited me to the pub for a drink right on 'arsenic hour' (If you are a mum, you know), so I cheerfully said, "Just give me a minute while I get the kids' shoes on and we'll be ready." He got the message.

I also learned to 'disown' my kids as (male) clients wouldn't believe I could meet deadlines if they knew I had four kids (mums are the best multi taskers ever – we work late into the night if we need to!). Because phones were on the kitchen bench, there was often background noise – one day my girls roller-skated in as I took a call, the client asked, "Do you have kids?" I responded with, "Oh, I'm minding a couple today."

Just as my business was going well, I got really sick. An autoimmune disorder reared its ugly head. This wasn't just for a week or two; it was for a long time. At first this was an enormous shock – what the...? I don't get sick; I am a person with boundless energy! I take care of myself – if that's what you call rushing to yoga class between deadlines, meetings, kids' activities and growing or shopping for organic veggies.

For more than six months, I could barely walk to the letterbox, I was so weak. I needed to earn an income, but I couldn't go out and see clients and I didn't have the energy to stay up late and work, so I sent an article in to The Age (Melbourne's big newspaper).

The editor called and said he was printing my article and asked if I could write more. An editor for a rival paper saw my work and also called me – could I write some features for him? I asked what topics and luckily he wanted health, education or family articles (Whew! Not politics or finance, thank goddess). Soon I was also writing for the feminist page of The Age. Ironically, I was grateful there wasn't Zoom back then, as I discussed the feminist perspective of King Lear with the editor, with a toddler latched on my boob.

Soon, other editors and publishers saw my work and I started writing for magazines on health, education, women's issues, and family topics.

My boys were now in high school, the girls were old enough to run their own baths and tie their own shoelaces. They were still home-schooled, and things were going smoothly despite my health challenges. I was feeling better but was still having difficulty pacing myself. On days I felt well, I would race around doing everything, only to crash because I had pushed myself too hard.
Then I fell pregnant!

I was overwhelmed at the prospect of another baby – the first 4 kids were 10 years apart – with the oldest boys now almost 16 and 18. I thought, how the bloody hell will I find the energy to push a baby out? But as my pregnancy progressed, I became healthier, and healthier. My energy came back, and I felt great. It turns out that autoimmune disorders can go into remission during pregnancy. I was lucky.

Born in the nineties, our 'bonus baby' is a 'digital native' – the first generation to have been born in the internet age.

The internet is a wonderful resource. It has brought so much information out of the ivory towers of academia. This gives us options; we can do our own research and make informed choices. But it's a double-edged sword.

As access to information and reliance on 'Dr Google' increased, I started to see more and more mothers doubting themselves. Another generation of women stopped trusting their intuition and innate wisdom. Instead, they looked outside for answers and handed over their parenting power to 'experts', many of whom have no health or early childhood backgrounds but are simply 'influencers' or have created their own titles, from various styles of 'baby sleep trainer' to 'breastfeeding mentor' or 'coach.'

During this time, feeling healthy again, I trained as an Infant Massage Instructor and an internationally Certified Lactation Consultant. I visited new mums in their homes, supporting them through breastfeeding difficulties, I taught infant massage to new parents at a local hospital and in private classes. I was immersed anew in the new parent and baby world.

I was worried and saddened that perfectly competent women doing a great job nurturing their babies were becoming more and more anxious, so I approached a book publisher about an idea I had. She said, "We don't do parenting books." However, she agreed to check out a one-page proposal and recommend another publisher. Within a week, she called me back and said, "We want to publish your book," and invited me to lunch.

This was the first version of my book, 'Parenting by Heart'.

I wrote '100 Ways to Calm the Crying', then moved to Penguin Australia as my publisher (now Penguin Random House) who took on my back titles. I wrote more books – a new and much bigger edition of 'Parenting by Heart',

'Sleeping Like a Baby', which has also been revised recently in a second edition and 'Toddler Tactics', for parents struggling without support to nurture gently as their little bundle in the bunny rug becomes an adventurous little explorer.

As my books became popular, I received regular media guest invitations – I love live radio and TV because it can't be edited. While being interviewed about a study that showed around 80% of Australian parents thought it was OK to smack toddlers, I strongly disagreed. The host argued, "But what about when you just can't get through to them?" I asked him, "What if you can't get through to your wife, would you hit her?"

I was invited to speak at events for parents and health professionals, in Australia, New Zealand and the United States. I held my own talks, in libraries at first and later hired hotel venues which became packed out and I was also invited to present a TEDx talk (Surrender is Not a Dirty Word).

During the pandemic, I pivoted from in-person events to offering webinars and virtual workshops and master-classes for parents and professionals and I started a podcast called 'Tits Up' to share free information. I also do guest podcast interviews, reaching a wider audience. With restrictions lifted, I am being booked to do in-person talks again.

**Here are my public speaking tips:**

**Just do it** – start small, hire a room in a local library; do a webinar. It doesn't matter how small your audience is, sometimes an intimate talk with a smaller group whose needs you are meeting can be gold. It's all practice and people you influence will talk about you; this helps promote you as a speaker and grow future audiences.

**Mingle and meet the audience** – circulate and chat briefly to people before your talk, this will help you relax, and people will feel connected so they will pay attention as you talk.

**Give, Give, Get** – be generous by doing free talks to volunteer groups and sharing information freely on social media, in blog posts or on podcasts. This means you will be sowing seeds that get you invitations to speak to more audiences. You will also get good testimonials.

I've demonstrated throughout my life that I'm proud to be loud. I've used my voice and the written word to advocate for myself, my kids, and mothers and babies. Never be afraid to speak up, for yourself and for the rights of others.

inkedin.com/in/pinky-mckay-04910a203

facebook.com/pinky.mckay.fanpage

@pinkymckayofficial

pinkymckay.com/blog

pinkymckay.com
boobiefoods.com.au

Connect with me

Chapter 9

# Becoming Free To Be Me

**Rachel Anastasi**
*Global Keynote Speaker, Coach, Author, NLP practitioner,
Psychosomatic Therapist & Teacher, Medium/Intuitive*

## About The Author: Rachel Anastasi

Rachel Amy Anastasi has a passion for Love, Freedom, Inner Security, Empower meant, Purpose, Sexuality, Embody meant, Abundance, Entrepreneurship, Ritual, Alchemy, Human Relating and Magic. Rachel started her first business, Free To Be Me Life Coaching, at age twenty one. In her first year of business, she lived in a seven tonne truck and drove the entire perimeter of Australia coaching, mentoring, teaching and speaking

Rachel returned to buy her first property and run transformational retreats from her lounge room and made a six figure profit in her second year of business.

Becoming the coaches coach, she loves teaching others how to be the most self-expressed version of themselves they can be.

Rachel has a passion for property development and was a self made millionaire by age thirty with a property portfolio she loves and gets super excited about sleeping in her van in nature, cooking on a fire under the stars and living out of a backpack.

Travelling the world, empowering thousands of people from all walks of life, empowering transformational results and sharing with others that we are BE ing at the source of our own lives.

Rachel has created four editions of her own magazine, been a published author, international speaker, coached top CEOs, interviewed celebrities on the red carpet, started her own wellness centre and volunteered extensively at women's shelters, AIDs centres in Africa and has served soup to the needy on the steps of an iconic train station in Melbourne.

Rachel is a coach, speaker, author, NLP practitioner, hypnotherapist, Psychosomatic therapist and teacher of nationally accredited certification, intuitive, medium, bodyworker and a unique, magical being who will move, touch and inspire you.

Rachel has lived her life like wild fire: "Let's take love on the run."

*Freedom of full self expression and an open heart to the art of human relating*

When I was sixteen years old, I desperately wanted to experience intimacy and love and when the new guy at school showed interest in me, I fell for him and we were together for three years.

I lost my virginity to him in the dark at a sleepover on my friend's bedroom floor surrounded by others. I felt I couldn't find the voice to say NO and I stayed because I was grateful that he wanted me.

I was spat on, I was strangled and held out over a balcony at the local club in a fit of jealousy and I stayed because I loved him.

I was lied to, cheated on, I had a key run down the side of my new car that I had saved for and I stayed because I thought I must deserve it.

Little did I know that I was running an underlying program and this relationship fed perfectly into it.

I was gathering evidence for a character that I invented in childhood, in moments of stress and had become a default program, an already and always way of being.

I was able to tell myself, "See…here is more evidence that there is 'something wrong with you,'" and I continued to feel like a victim and then, of course, I got to play the martyr because I stayed to 'help him'.

You see, when I was a child, I created the story that I was worthless, that there was something wrong with me and that I did not deserve to have what I wanted in life.
To compensate, I created the belief that in order to be loved, I had to be a good girl, be happy all of the time and try really hard to please people.

To honour my good girl tendencies, I kept my challenges all secret, worked harder at school, became a school captain, got the top marks I needed to get into my desired university course, got that extra job after school and on the outside, I was seen to be a high achieving, very successful, outspoken, confident person.

At age nineteen, I experienced pregnancy and had a procedure to end it in secret, terrified that this would leave a 'black mark' on my life. I went through the experience alone and felt devastated that I may disappoint my parents.

Behind closed doors, I was really not coping well with life.

I felt like a blow-up doll, like a prostitute.

I was prostituting myself to the masks I was wearing.

I was literally selling myself to the identity I had created and I had totally bought into it.

I felt like I was playing many different characters, wearing many masks and I had no idea who I was. I had not been to the depths of myself.

I left university one year into the degree. I felt that I needed to find the meaning of life and figure it out; I needed to find myself. I travelled to Europe on my own at age nineteen and remained there for two years, having the absolute time of my life but not really feeling any closer to 'finding myself'.

Upon my return, I was not sure what my life was for, why I was here; I felt as if I did not have a purpose in life. I felt desperate to seek and find my career path and what I wanted to do with my life.

I had a lot that I wanted to share.

I knew that finding and liberating my own unique voice and spirit was imperative to my own full fill meant and happiness.

This began a pursuit to become Free To Be Me, which would become the name of my first business, launched at age twenty one.

I returned to study and became immersed in the world of human behaviour, brain functionality, language patterns and my huge passion for human relating, communication and the intimacy that I craved became fed by being with people in their depths and in their truth. I was starting to feel so empowered within myself and such a huge level of acceptance and love for myself and I wanted everyone to experience the same. My inner security was developing.

It all began after attending my first personal development course and when I went along to the information session that started it all, sitting in that room, all of a sudden, I realised (real eyes) that there were other people just like me.

They were sad too.

They were angry too.

They felt lost too.

I was so happy to finally feel like maybe there wasn't something wrong with me and that it was okay that I was challenged and that I did not feel worthy.

I realised that there is no intrinsic purpose to life and that it was up to me to create purpose full endeavours for myself and my life and invent new realms of possibility that allowed my truest self expression to be experienced.

Finding myself was redundant and creating and inventing myself became my focus.

**EGO IS NECESSARY FOR OUR SURVIVAL BUT THE TRUTH OF WHO WE REALLY ARE IS, WE ARE INFINITE POSSIBILITIES AND POTENTIALITIES**

Every human being has an "unanswerable question".

I feel that the core question of every human being is, "am I loved?" ("do you love me?" "am I loveable?")

This question ensures our survival and keeps our egos in place as we will do whatever it takes to remain part of the herd.

There is a core fear that underlies this question and that is the fear of not being loved. Keeping this fear in place is an act of survival. The fight or flight mechanism of the brain is governed by this fear.

What is an unanswerable question? A question that can never be answered and is always going to remain unanswerable, like a thirst that can never be satiated.

I can produce as many answers to this question as I like and I will still continue to hold the question "am I loved?" and seek evidence to prove to myself that I am or that I am not depending on my belief.

Holding this question as a constant enquiry, drives egoic behavior and keeps certain ways of being in place. Whenever I relate to myself as unlovable and seek to answer the question "do you love me?" I will continue to be whoever I feel I need to be 'in order' to be loved.

In childhood, certain characters get created—characters that ensure we are safe, loved and part of the tribe and then we relate to ourselves as those characters, when actually we have the infinite potential to be anything and everything

The fear of not being loved had me be obedient to my dad and listen to what I perceived to be put downs from family, it had me stay silent when my nana died at age seven, scared that the love I had inside would hurt me if I expressed it, it had me placate the friends at primary school that I felt bullied by for years, it had me stay silent when I was in sexually dishonoring experiences that I did not consent to, it drove me to be that 'high achiever' and aim to be everything to everyone and avoid letting anyone down.

It was the fear of not being loved and the question "am I loved" and its unanswerable nature that had me keep showing up over and over, in ways to seek that love but no matter what I did, I still felt like it was never enough.

I kept this character alive; that ensured my 'survival' because there was popularity in the crowd for that character and I knew how to be that character.

Once I figured out that there was a whole part of my brain designed to keep me safe by keeping these programs running, I was able to disappear the trauma. It was my own stories, my own beliefs and my own choices that were at the source of my results. I chose to let it go. I chose to kill off that character. I chose to reprogram my neurology.

I chose to create new ways of being and call forward new paradigms from my imagination. I practiced choosing my state and leading my own results. When choosing our state, we are utilising a way of operating that insists we are coming from a space of already achieved. By being who I would be if I already had the results I imagined, I started to experience new states. I was being who I wanted to be and then doing the actions in alignment with those ways of being and then I was having new and breakthrough results that were a triumph over the past stories.

## BE- DO- HAVE

Our brains have stored everything that we have ever seen, felt, heard, tasted and experienced at an unconscious level. Our body has stored every physical experience and every emotion at a cellular level. Our DNA is literally woven out of our life's experiences and then everything that is happening in the now is seen through the filter of the past and felt through the filter of the past.

This is how our brains work, however the thing is that we are always experiencing the past over and over again, in our current experiences, even if they are completely different because it is the same old neurology and the same old psychology/physiology that is being used to have the experience with.

The brain must change and the body must change to be able to have a different experience. Otherwise, the circumstances can be completely different but the body and mind will recreate the same experience.

To create truly different results in my life, I knew I needed to shift things radically and I went on many adventures physically, emotionally, mentally, sexually and spiritually in my quest to feel free to be me.

A friend said to me, so many people would love to have your level of freedom to be honest. That really hit me because it is true that I am so willing to be honest about the way that I choose to live my life because it's the only access that I have to freedom.

'I AM' the only access to freedom that I have.

If I don't amplify my truth then I am going to be living at odds with my own freedom.

The freedom to be, is the key to happiness.

Happiness is a state and by be ing free to flow and amplify our own truth and honest nature we can thrive and experience feelings of euphoria and vitality and arousal because we are nothing but our senses. Our senses are the gateway and access to our freedom.

As animals we are governed by our needs and our desires yet as human beings we have told ourselves that it is not okay to only be driven by this. We have somehow told ourselves that there must be some logic or intellect behind our actions otherwise they are not viable.

The more I allow my senses to be my guide, the more in tune I become and I am able to sensitise myself to energies that are around me.

**INTIMACY EXISTS IN THE MOMEMT OF NOW, IN THE 'NOT KNOWING'**

When we allow the future to call us forward, new ways of being can be experienced in the spontaneity and the intimacy of the moment.
I have felt so deeply in my lifetime. I relate to myself as quite an intense person. My experiences are never surface level. I like to delve in. My body has strong emotional reactions and responses. I like it and I think that it is healthy. If there is an emotion to feel, fill your body up with it completely and allow yourself to fully feel each emotion and then you are able to release the emotion. Energy in motion

My uncle died when I was in my final year of primary school, he was twenty nine years old and he was killed in a motorcycle accident. I already knew that life was not forever but I did not know what it meant to lose someone young. There was a part of me that wad so sad because he was my uncle and there was also a part of me that knew that I did not even know him at all and therefore it felt weird that I was so sad.

The lost opportunity was again the notion that somehow, I knew that there was something else, some other possibility that had not come to fruition.

Can we ever know someone?

The more we 'know' someone, the more we are relating to them from the past.

Each moment with someone is intimacy. As intimate as we can ever be, is, right now in this moment because that is the only moment we have.

Getting to know someone better is actually dragging with you the beliefs about them given by the past and then making the present correlate with those beliefs which is therefore shaping the individual in that moment and not allowing them the freedom to show up however they want to.

Intimacy is receiving ourselves and each other and the connection from a space of nothing because that allows the true depth and the true connection to that person and how they are showing up in that moment. How they want to be received in the now, rather than how you 'know' them to be.

Where does someone else finish and where do you begin? We all only exist in our perception of ourselves and each other

When we fall in love with someone else aren't we just falling in love with ourselves?

When we seek to 'know' someone better, to know them deeper, maybe we are just missing a depth with ourselves in that moment. There is something we feel we do not have access to. To keep coming from a space of nothing is to live in a purely creative space and our own evolution and our connection to others becomes a limitless work of art and soul.

## I AM AT THE SOURCE OF HOW MY WORLD OCCURS FOR ME

It really helps me to remember that I am constantly creating everything. I don't know about you but for me that makes me feel so much better. Like things can show up as so challenging and I can feel like everything is falling apart and then I have the thought that I am creating this, that I am drawing it in being that way. That I am manifesting this. That this is the way that it is supposed to be for me…and then all of a sudden it does seem like this is manageable, like this is something that I must be able to deal with.

That I can deal with and that everything is going to be okay.

There must be some bigger picture here.

Do I know this to be true?

Well, no, I don't, however this belief helps me so much, and not only that, it makes sense to me. If I am the only one who exists in my universe and everyone else is a projection of me then I am writing the script as we speak.

It cannot be a coincidence how things are unravelling.

Sure, there is cause and effect—I take an action and it causes an effect and this is intermingled in a complicated and complex intricate web with the trillions of other people causing effects all over the world, however there must be some rhyme to it.

Surely if it was all completely random, we would have spontaneously combusted by now with the sheer volume of experiences clashing together.
I believe that we are here to engage with our innate gifts and share them.

It can be seen that when we step fully into our own power that there is an absence of humility. Humble was already built into our existence through wrangling these beautiful bodies we have. I believe that life is all about liberating the spirit and truly connecting with our higher calling, which has been perfectly intertwined in the gifts that we have been gifted and we naturally desire to connect with others through those gifts.

When we all allow ourselves and each other to shine then we get to walk the path that we are designed to walk and we all fit together like a puzzle. It is a golden weave that is woven in every second of every moment of every cell in our DNA in the invisible web that surrounds us. It is the golden thread that bonds existence.

When we are sharing our unique gifts, that is also a truly humbling experience. I have been bought to tears so many times when I have witnessed others sharing their true god-given gifts and engaging with the true essence of who they really are.

I see absolutely nothing but humility in these moments. I do not believe that owning stuff and having wealth, so to speak does not make you any less humble because I believe that when we are engaging with what we are truly here to do then we are already coming from a space of humility and service. We are here to be in commune and to come together in common unity to share our gifts with each other and to each shine individually and as a collective.

I feel that each of us came to this planet to experience something and our life will deliver exactly what it is we were meant to go through to have that experience. This is why it is ultimately an act of love and an act of rebellion to be your own truth, the way and the light.

My journey has been about liberating my voice and feeling safe to be in my body with an open heart to all that life has to offer. To be in the moment and give myself over to the moments fully. To feel empowered physically, sexually, emotionally, mentally, spiritually, energetically and to allow my five senses to connect me to the magic of each moment.

**Be Here Now**

'Be here now' are three little words and even the word HERE holds so much power when placed in between the words BE and NOW. For me this simple little phrase evokes big feelings. The BEing is where life IS.
We live IN love and we are BE ing in love.

With every single breath we take, we linger between life and death.

I truly do feel that the final breath in life is equally as important as the first breath, and to be honest, how can we differentiate any breath as any more or less important than another, as each and every breath is of equal importance and relevance and maintains the consistency of life.

Our life's experiences are perfect, whole and complete just the way that they are and just the way that they are not.

I have got to be true to myself.

Chapter 10

# A Man is Not a Financial Plan

**Sally Prowse**
*Global Keynote Speaker, Founder and CEO Sandcastle Finance*

## About The Author: Sally Prowse

Sally Prowse's dedication to empowering women in their financial and investment endeavours has driven her career as a finance broker. She draws from both her personal experiences and her continuous pursuit of knowledge in the field of finance to guide and inspire others. Over the years, she has gained not only professional qualifications but also personal wisdom that she generously shares with her clients.

As Sally continues to empower women and equip them with the knowledge and tools to achieve financial independence, her personal journey stands as a testament to the transformative power of self-belief, resilience, and a commitment to helping others.

Her story is that of a woman who has not only overcome great adversity but is determined to ensure that others can do the same, proving that financial security and independence are within reach for anyone willing to take charge of their own destiny.

• • • •

When I arrived home, the house felt unusually empty. Soon, my mother returned, and I inquired about my father's whereabouts. Her response left me bewildered – she had no idea where he was. This was a highly unusual situation.

I had my mid-year exams beginning the following day, and I was deeply engrossed in my studies. It was around 9 pm when my mother entered my room, asking if I needed anything from our computer. I replied, "No, why?" Her response took me by surprise – "Your bloody father!" My mother rarely used profanity. She told me she would be back shortly.

It was June 1992, and I was 20 years old. My life, on the surface, seemed perfect. My parents appeared to have a happy marriage, and I had two beautiful sisters. I had received an education at one of Sydney's best schools, had an amazing group of girlfriends, and a wonderful boyfriend. We lived in a spacious home in Sydney's upper North Shore.

There was some commotion outside my bedroom about 30 minutes later, and I overheard raised voices saying, "He's gone." After the voices subsided, my mother re-entered my room, and in that moment, my life changed forever.

My father had been apprehended red-handed while attempting to scam the sale of an estate in Wahroonga, an affluent suburb in Sydney's upper North Shore. He had posed as a real estate agent trying to sell a deceased estate. This wasn't the first time my father had been entangled with the law due to fraudulent activity. During the afternoon, the police had interrogated him at the station. He'd convinced them that he had information at his house, so they brought him home to search through his papers.

According to my father's account, the police discovered some cash in his filing cabinet and allowed him ten minutes to locate important documents. Seizing the opportunity, my father promptly got into a rented car and drove away. I wouldn't see him again until my 21st birthday, six months later.

My mother came and informed me that my father had "gone," and I couldn't fully grasp the implications. I knew I had exams the next day. Needless to say, the exams were postponed as we faced a harsh reality – we had no money, and we would have to move. My younger sister was in the middle of her HSC trials, and my little sister was in the USA. As the eldest child, I had no choice but to step up.

My mother had grown up in an environment where children were shielded from the harsh truth, whatever it involved. My uncle came to the rescue, and within a month, we had packed up our enormous three-storey, six-bedroom home and relocated to Queensland, where my uncle provided a three-bedroom villa for us. He also helped my mother find a job in real estate.

I couldn't wait to leave Queensland – my life was in Sydney. My younger sister returned from her year-long exchange in the US. We rerouted her flight to the Gold Coast, where we had to recount the unravelling of our lives to her. She had just turned 17. A week after her return, I left the Gold Coast and I moved in with my then-boyfriend's family back in Sydney.

I was pursuing a business degree and quickly learned that I was on my own from that point. My father had always told me he would take care of me. However, this wasn't the first time my father had had legal troubles. He always insisted he was innocent and I didn't want to face the painful truth.

It took me until I was 40, with three children of my own and happily married, to understand that we need to seize control of our own destiny, whatever that may entail. We can't blame others – we have one life, and as women, we must take charge of our financial future.

There were plenty of red flags; my father was taken away just before my 10th birthday for fraud and arson and spent 11 months away from us. I'll never forget the first day my mother took her three daughters to visit their father in jail. We hadn't seen him for six weeks, and he had been taken away just before Christmas.

We were dressed in our best outfits, in the jail's waiting room. I remember feeling so out of place. We were searched by the guards and then sat among other families of criminals until they allowed us to see our dad. The visit was highly traumatic, but it was a contact visit where we could touch and hug our father while he assured us that everything would be okay. By the end of the day, it felt like it was. Believing that things will be okay goes a long way to life actually turning out okay.

Eventually, my father was released 11 months later and I was overjoyed that he was home. That Christmas, my mother had to decide between her immediate family and my father. Looking back, she made the unfortunate choice to stay with my father because she felt she had no other option. Mum hadn't worked for over a decade, and believed she was reliant on my father for survival. This scenario is all too common, where women remain in marriages because they don't believe they can make it on their own. It's crucial for women to understand that they always have a choice.

While I was in school, my mother appeared to have a charmed life from the outside. She was engaged in pottery classes, lunches, tennis, and socializing. She was always there for us girls; I can't recall a time growing up when my mother wasn't present.

I was fortunate enough to start my high school years at a private girls' school in Year 7, only 12 months after my father was released from prison. Reflecting on it, my father must have been an incredibly convincing salesperson because he soon acquired a hotel in Canberra. He spent most weekdays in Canberra and returned home on weekends. It's still a mystery to me how someone who had lost so much could acquire a hotel only 12 months later.

My father relished being in charge of the hotel. He wanted to relocate our family to Canberra, but I was determined not to move – I was 13, and I loved my school, my life, and friends in Sydney.

Shortly after he was released from prison, we moved from the family home in St Ives to a more extensive residence in Turramurra in 1985. This home only lasted for four years, and I remember coming home from school one day to find we couldn't enter the house. There was some unexplained "issue with the mortgage payment," and we sold the house in 1989, believing we were moving on to better things. My father never owned another house after that.

The following years became a blur. After finishing school, I was offered a cadetship with Deloitte while studying at university. The year I left school, we went on our first family overseas trip to Canada before I began my working career.

The next Christmas, my parents booked another overseas trip for the five of us. Two days before we were due to fly out, my father gathered us in the dining room to explain that he couldn't leave the country as his passport had been confiscated. I was heartbroken that my father wouldn't be spending Christmas with us. As it turned out, I would never spend another Christmas with my father until I had a family of my own. My mum and my sisters left my father home alone for that January while they enjoyed an overseas holiday.

Later that year, my father supposedly got his passport back. My mother and he planned a trip to South America; there was some "deal" happening in Panama in October 1991. My sister and I were going to be left home alone for a couple of weeks – the first time ever. Our eager party planning was quickly thwarted as my mother unexpectedly returned home alone. Our father had been caught trying to fly out of the country on a fake passport, and off he went to prison again.

I received a call from my father from prison, telling me that I needed to step up and not go overseas, as he wasn't there. Defiantly, I refused to stay home and instead left for the three-month holiday – after all, I had saved up for it, over the past two years. My family would never be the same – I left my middle sister and my mother to have Christmas on their own, with my father in prison and my baby sister in the US.

While traveling in Europe, I received a fax from my father saying that he was now home again. I was returning home the next month, and I was excited that our family would all be together once more. I came home in February 1992 to find out that my father's brief release from prison hadn't lasted long. He had been released on bail after convincing his cellmate, Howard Hilton, who was jailed for bribing the NSW prisons minister to let his clients out early, to put up his own house as bail. The deal was that my father was going to write a book and had already sold the rights. Hilton would receive some of the proceeds if he could use his home as security.

However, it wasn't long before Hilton discovered the truth – there was no book deal. He withdrew his house as security, resulting in my father being sent back to prison just before I returned home, once again arriving to no father in the house.

My father soon had a new plan – his next target became my boyfriend's parents. After convincing them to visit him in jail, he persuaded them to put up their home as security so he could be released once again. This time, he promised an all-expenses-paid, around-the-world tour. This tour was all arranged on his letterhead via his computer, and it took place in March 1992, three months before he would vanish from the family home for good. The bad news was that around this time, I'd chosen to break up with my then-boyfriend, run off with his best friend, and my father ran away from the police – not the most glorious period in my life.

In September during the university break in 1992, my boyfriend and I drove to the Gold Coast to visit my mother and baby sister. My father had been on the run since that evening three months before. On my first day at my mother's new home, I discovered numerous letters that my father had written. He expressed remorse, love, and his desire for us to write to him. When my mother returned, I demanded an explanation of the situation as we hadn't all been together since our world fell apart in June. My mother sat us three girls down and showed us all the letters. He had a P.O. Box in Brisbane where he implored us to write to him, and we all did. I was relieved to learn that my father was alive and well, and I started writing to him.

In the meantime, another tragedy was unfolding before our eyes. My younger sister had lost nearly 15 kilograms since I had last seen her in June. She was showing signs of anorexia that would stay with her for the next six years. When we left the Gold Coast and returned to Sydney, I continued to write to my father.

A couple of months later, I'd still not heard from my father and was living with my boyfriend and his family. To my surprise, one day he called. My boyfriend's sister was training to be a police officer and my father was on the run, so I was scared of being watched and compromising my living situation. We had a brief conversation during which he assured me that everything would be okay, that he missed us all and wanted to see us. He said he would send us plane tickets under false names and fly us to Melbourne to celebrate my 21st birthday.

So, the three of us flew to Melbourne and checked into a fancy hotel under false names. Soon there was a knock at the door, and in walked our father with apologies, cash, and abundant promises.

Upon seeing my little sister, whom he hadn't seen since she left for America 18 months earlier, he was devastated by how much weight she had lost. We enjoyed three days of luxury with cash lavished on us and promises of how he would take care of us. Each of us was given a cash card with a promise of access to $10,000, which was a significant amount in 1992. We returned home, sworn to secrecy – my father's plan had worked. We believed our father had an endless supply of cash and could continue living on the run. We had no idea how naïve we were.

Since this little holiday worked so well, we received tickets to do it all over again six weeks later. This time, though, my little sister would first spend some "special" time with my father before my other sister and I joined them for another family reunion. My father intended to "fix" her and her eating disorder. They spent a few days in Tasmania before we were to join them in Melbourne. As we were getting ready to go to the airport, we received a call from my little sister – "Dad's been caught at the bank and arrested." Time was up. His seven months on the run had ended. He had been going to different banks daily, withdrawing cash, and this time he was caught. We told my sister to get on the next flight home. When we tried to withdraw the promised funds from our cash cards, we found all the money was frozen. My father was in a lot of trouble.

The following night, my boyfriend and I tuned in to the late news, and there, on the TV screens, was a picture of my father plastered across the broadcast. The headline read:

**ELUSIVE CARVER OUT THE WINDOW!**

"In an extraordinary turn of events, Phillip Kingston Carver, the man allegedly involved in the aborted $132 million dollar sale of Occidental and Regal Life escaped from police custody, just 24 hours after being apprehended!" the journalist dramatically reported.

That was the breaking point; I was frozen with a mix of emotions. Shame, embarrassment, betrayal, and the full, harsh realization that my father would never truly be there to look after me. I knew I was on my own. In an attempt to escape the constant headlines, my boyfriend and I headed down to the south coast, where we camped for a week until the news died down. Looking back, I'm grateful that there was no social media back then. However, I couldn't shake the shame of having a father in jail for at least the next decade. I was angry at myself for trusting him and angry at him for letting me down.

For the next four years, my father remained imprisoned in Victoria. I visited him whenever I could, and he would call me every Sunday morning. He always talked about how, once he got out, he would make amends, support us, and take care of us. Sadly, I believed him for far too long.

In 1996, my boyfriend proposed to me, and we planned our wedding for March 1997. My father was supposed to be released in January 1997 and had promised to pay for the wedding. However, when the time came, he was released from the Victorian prison system only to be promptly arrested again by the NSW authorities. Despite my friends constantly warning me that my father was a liar and wouldn't make it to the wedding, I didn't want to believe them. Though my head knew they were right, my heart clung to hope.

I appeared at the hearing that day at the district court, hoping it was all a mistake, but my father couldn't even look at me. The police informed me that he knew he would be remanded in custody by NSW as soon as he was released from the Victorian prison system. This meant he wouldn't be there for my wedding, and he wouldn't be paying for it. The wedding date was moved to May as we tried to come up with a plan. We were on our own.

Our wedding finally took place on May 10th, and I'm still happily married. My husband has been my rock throughout these tumultuous years, and I consider myself lucky to have him in my life.

On December 9, 2000, my father was finally released for good. My eldest child was just 9 weeks old. My sister and my mother picked him up from Bathurst jail, welcoming him with open arms into our home. He stayed for no more than three weeks, moving in with a friend who owned an apartment at Coogee. This friend, Paul,[1] fell victim to another of my father's tall tales, believing he would receive a $1,000,000 check any day. In early 2003, he visited my husband and me, presenting piles of evidence that proved my father's deceit. It was one of the final straws, and over the next decade, our relationship remained tumultuous. It was when I turned 40 that I decided I could no longer have him in my life. This period also marked my decision to take control of my financial life.

With my youngest child starting school, I had the time to dedicate myself to a career as a finance broker, working in a financial planning firm. I began learning about goal setting and how property investment could generate passive income in retirement. Having taken time away from the workforce to raise my family, I understood the impact on my family's finances.

It wasn't until I started my own business in 2014 that I recognized the urgent need to educate women about their financial future. My initial clients were friends going through divorces, and like me, they had relied on the men in their lives for financial matters. In their 40s, many of my friends saw their wealth reduced by half due to divorce. I still grappled with self-doubt, as my father was a fraud, and I questioned my authority to educate others. I believed I had to master financial independence myself before guiding others.

I was constantly reading books on passive income from authors like Margaret Lomas, Jan Somers, and Terry Ryder, and I applied some of their principles to my life. Starting my business with a coach, I continued to seek mentorship to help me with my business. I realized the importance of goal setting, both in personal and business life. I began to believe that financial freedom was attainable through property investment and strategic planning.

Over the last five years, I have transformed my mindset and beliefs about money through authors like Bob Proctor, Joe Vitale, David Schwatz, and Gabrielle Bernstein. Earlier this year, I asked my mother about her feelings regarding money. She revealed that she always believed she would be fine, and indeed, she has been. Celebrating her 80th birthday this year and getting married, she is an incredible woman. Despite having a narcissistic father, I am fortunate to have an amazing mother.

Today, my mission is to educate others about their money mindset and how anyone, with the help of the right resources, can build a passive income for their future. Relying solely on others for financial security is not an option, and I firmly believe that "A Man is not a Financial Plan."

My journey serves as a testament to the power of self-belief, resilience, and commitment to helping others.

sandcastlefinance.com.au

linkedin.com/in/sallyprowse

facebook.com/sandcastlefinance

@sandcastlefinance

Connect with me

Chapter 11

# Your Life, Your Purpose, Your Pace

**Priya Ravindra Kalyanimath**
*Global Keynote Speaker, Founder and CEO, Punar, Company Director -GAICD*

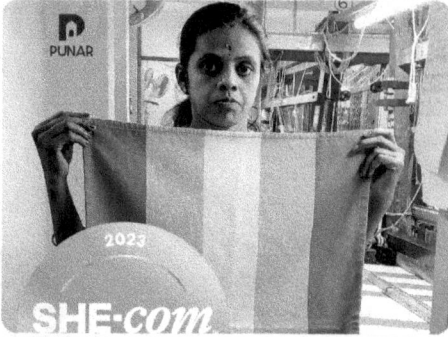

## About The Author: Priya Ravindra Kalyanimath

Priya Ravindra is the Founder and CEO of Punar, an Award winning ethical and sustainable gifting company based in Melbourne. Priya has been leading and advocating gender diversity and equal opportunity initiatives for women since 2002. Her vision is to help women rise.

By launching Punar she is aiming to bring this vision to fruition.

Punar artisans, predominantly skilled women weavers in India, transform recycled yarn sourced from landfill textile waste into premium handloom fabrics, crafting meaningful, ethically made gifts.

Priya's unwavering commitment to ethics, sustainability, and empowering these artisans has left an indelible mark on the corporate and business gifting landscape. Under her guidance, Punar stands as a beacon of hope, not only for the artisans but also for their entire communities.

Priya, an accredited company director with a GAICD certification, brings a wealth of experience, having successfully led multi-million-dollar technology and business transformation projects in both the public and private sectors. She has further contributed to the governance of various organizations by serving on two boards for over five years.

A lifelong learner, Priya is a recipient of University Chancellor's Awards and numerous scholarships, reflecting her enduring dedication to personal and professional growth.

With her debut as an author, Priya aims to share her inspiring journey, her passion for uplifting women, and the remarkable story of Punar's ethical and sustainable mission with the world.

She enjoys traveling, listening to Huberman Lab Podcasts, reading and keeps fit with strength training & yoga.

• • • • •

Have you ever wondered how the world might be if gender equality and inclusion was woven into every fabric of our being? I have often wondered about it, the only answer I can think of right now - it doesn't exist yet, so why not change the status quo. I get it, this world isn't a fairytale however, rather than being a by stander, I am choosing to take actions like most of you. My actions are to create a better world that is based on gender diversity, equality, and inclusion. My vision is to help women rise and I want to rise with them.

My name is Priya. I am proud of my heritage and South Indian roots. I am an Australian, calling this beautiful land my home for nearly 24 years. Mysore, India, a city with a storied past and a thriving cultural scene is where I started life.

My hometown air is fragrant with sandalwood and the distant chimes of temple bells can be heard in the nights. I enjoyed bucolic childhood holidays at my paternal grandparent's village located in the stunning hilly area called Western Ghats, a UNESCO World Heritage Site. My connection with earth and respect for nature runs deep, my happy place is lush green surroundings. I am a big believer in the concept of global village. Today, I am proud to say that I am building a global community of women determined to create a better world.

Through the lens of a seven-year-old: As a child in India, I used to wonder why people outside my family often treated women differently. Whether it was subtle actions, remarks making women feel inferior, uncomfortable, or blatant disrespect towards women and girl child in general, it made me angry, and I always vowed to myself "when I get bigger, I am not going to let it happen".

This little girl wanted to the girl who changes what wasn't right. True, I haven't been on receiving end of this behaviour but witnessing these as a child leaves a mark. I knew deep down that I was going to do something to change this accepted norm.

Let me venture into a topic deemed uncomfortable by some, not me. This incident occurred when I was 13 and still living in India. In India, women are often encouraged to rest when they commence menstrual cycle and advised not to enter prayer rooms or temples. Yes, there is some science to this notion, although not explained clearly but passed on merely as "rules" that women are encouraged to abide by.

My curious mind was wondering if women are not allowed to pray, be in prayer rooms or go to temples, how we can have idols of goddesses in our prayer room all year round. Don't they have periods and what is so wrong about having periods, why this should stop women from doing things. I asked my smart and sassy maternal grandma, "Ajji (grand ma) doesn't Goddess Lakshmi (Goddess of wealth in Hindu religion) get periods? Why are goddesses in the prayer room all year round? This rule does not make much sense."

Instead of dictating rules, my maternal grandmother explained to me in simple terms, "it's just a lifestyle suggestion dear so that women can rest up. We all know periods can get uncomfortable and too bad, no one bothers to ask why and seek answers except you!" My grandmother chuckled and added, "Maybe these Goddesses have easy periods, they don't have any discomfort. Wouldn't it be great if all women on earth had easy menstrual cycles?"

A great practical and useful answer by a woman raised in a patriarchal society, a woman married off at 16 and a sassy soul that had patience of a mountain while dealing with her curious pestering grandchildren like me! I was blessed with incredibly intelligent grandmothers, both who loved me dearly and supported me unconditionally. My educated parents have never ever told me I couldn't do something because I was a girl. Yes, I am that lucky girl child, but we all know, it is not the same for countless girls in India. It is 2023, India is making progress with gender equality yet female infanticide, honour killing of women, forced arranged marriages and dowry deaths are still rampant. Is there hope? Certainly yes, however I am acutely aware that this is still a journey and we cannot stop yet.

My earliest role models were my parents and my grandmothers. My father is a lawyer and an incredible human. He always said to me "You can be yourself; be loud, be free and live your life". My father has a strong commitment to equality, inclusion, and women's rights. His beliefs were manifested in his deeds as well as words. No matter their socioeconomic standing or gender, I have witnessed him treating everyone with respect and dignity. My mother, a lecturer at a local university, exemplified discipline, and brilliance. She had this amazing talent for juggling her personal and professional lives in a way that made it appear effortless. She would always say, "We must do our best." She pushed me to achieve academic success while also growing as a person.

A bit more about my grandmothers, who were wise, clever, and strong. My maternal grandma enjoyed telling stories. She would tell me stories featuring powerful female characters, giving me the idea that girls and women could be heroes too. On the other hand, my paternal grandma was a strong, independent woman who travelled alone, learned how to use a mobile and send me text messages at the ripe age of 70. Trust me, these two were exceptions. The majority of older women in India never get to use their true voice, opinions or live their life on their own terms.

Like any child in India, I was strongly encouraged to focus on academic excellence. I did that, not because of parental or peer pressure; rather, because I was eager to learn and easy to teach. I want to admit that I am competitive, but it has never been about comparison, I compete to become the best version of myself. I am not the person who is interested in keeping up with the Joneses. Year 10 is a big deal in India. I scored 5th place in the exams taken by 150,000 plus students – I was on the television, interviewed by magazines, quoted in the newspapers and so on. My hard work was rewarded but I did struggle with the influx of attention. I am reflecting on this because it is so easy to assume that a person is ambitious because they want fame, popularity, and attention. Short answer: no, I am ambitious but that is not coupled with desire to be most popular or famous. I do what I do because I follow my calling.

Looking back, I can see that my upbringing was a jigsaw puzzle whose individual pieces all helped complete the person I am today. As I learned more about the societal norms that frequently excluded women, inclusion and equality became increasingly important to me. Not only did my parents and grandparents provide me love and an education, but they also gave me the freedom to be who I am today. They created the groundwork for me to build a successful, purposeful, and meaningful life. I took these teachings with me when it was time for me to leave Mysore and relocate to Australia. Armed with the wisdom of the individuals who mattered the most, I was prepared for the upcoming chapter.

**There she goes!! My move to Australia.**

Why are you sending your teenage daughter to Australia, that too all alone? This was the most frequently asked question my parents had to endure until the point the question changed to, "when is your daughter getting married?"

I can see that smile on most readers who understand what I am explaining. No matter which part of the world, these are such normalised questions and people have no qualms questioning other's life goals or ambitions, because how dare you defy the norm and not fit in a box? Add gender to the mix, we all know how many boxes women are expected to fit into!

Yes, moving to Australia as a teenager in early 2000 was a significant transition in my life's story, not just in terms of geography. When I made this decision, I was a teenager and at times it felt like taking a plunge into unchartered waters. I did my research, connected with reputable universities in Australia and trusted my intuition. My fascination towards technology prompted me to enrol in Bachelor of Electronics and Micro Engineering in Adelaide, South Australia. I had this dream that I would be working for a super tech company like Intel.

You see, I didn't land the engineering course I wanted in Mysore, so I wanted to explore other options. By now you may have figured out that I love to push myself and create my own path. Just in time, I went to an exhibition on Australian universities and decided to give Australia a go. Sure, I was sounding like a crazy teenager, and we had some deep discussions about this at home. But my parents believed in my crazy dream and supported my new adventure. I had my family's morals and support, so I never felt alone. They served as my compass as I navigated this new journey.

Australia was a completely different place from India in every aspect, including culture, geography, and climate. The sheer size of the land was the first thing that got my attention. I was used to being surrounded by people in India. In my hometown, communities were tight knit and everyone knew one another. The surroundings were vast, and the sky appeared to go on forever. It was thrilling yet slightly terrifying at the same time.

As a teenager, making friends and adapting to this fascinating place called Downunder were the new challenges I was expecting, but I wasn't prepared for the intensity of change in everyday life! I may have been pointed as a stubborn girl, but I call it committed and determined; it helps me get through tough days with a strong mindset. During stressful times, my go to has always been a quote from one of the greatest Indian philosophers, Swami Vivekananda: "Arise, awake! Stop not until your goal is reached." It assisted me in assimilating into a new culture while being loyal to myself.

As years passed in Adelaide, I was blessed with amazing friends, teachers and community of Indians in Adelaide who welcomed me into their homes as their own family member. Pursuing engineering meant I was one of the 4 girls in a class of 70 boys. We went on to third and fourth year of our bachelor's degree, yet I didn't see the change I was hoping for – the reality was that girls did not enrol in STEM courses like engineering. Although I had a wonderful group of young men in my class, you see me, and one of my dearest friends often discussed the lack of gender diversity in our classes. Hey, we wanted to talk about shoes and handbags along with signals and systems you know. Not just footy or night out plans!

When the opportunity came up to visit high schools in Adelaide metropolitan region and teach coding to kids, my lovely friend and I jumped with joy. We were the only two girls in the community engagement program, but we were determined to encourage girls to learn how to code and pursue engineering. Our efforts were rewarded with the University Chancellor's Award two years in a row. But I want to emphasise what drives me is my purpose, not awards. I appreciate the recognition, but I do not pursue initiatives with the ambition to end up with a trophy. My goal is to strive for gender equality and inclusion. This is still the same. I am not changing my stance no matter what anyone says – we know it is a long journey filled with challenges.

Fast forward few years, I relocated to Melbourne for work and personal reasons. My husband is a Melbournian plus I loved Melbourne and the shoes it can offer! Jokes aside, I moved because my plan was to move to Melbourne or Sydney eventually. In Melbourne, my corporate career was thriving. I completed my post graduate degree and had the opportunity to do some studies in Canada through a scholarship grant. I was elected to two boards as a board director. I had the privilege of serving on these boards for over five years. Following this, I completed the accredited Company Director course through Victorian Government scholarship for women leaders who are leading gender diversity initiatives within the community. Yes, I was living my dream life but only a few knew I was battling a serious health issue in private.

I am an endo warrior, I have stage 4 endometriosis which brings significant fertility challenges, not to mention the debilitating pain that affects quality of life. I felt like an utter failure, there were days so dark with no hope and the constant unwelcoming questions and unwanted advice from people who wanted me to focus on having a child not career. Well, I look around now in

2023, and I am glad most women are not putting up with these unwanted private questions about life choices like having children. I don't think we are fully out of the woods yet.

I was fortunate enough to find the right specialist and welcome my beautiful daughter in 2017, however it was one of the most difficult phases in my life. It made me think about millions of women in India and around the world, how often our voices and our pain are ignored or brushed off. My fertility journey only solidified my desire to help women rise to create a better world. I had time to deeply reflect on the challenges experienced by many women in India who come from complex backgrounds - they can't afford a home, good education, or healthcare for their children or family consistently. I know that many women in India are waiting to provide quality care for their children and their family. This was when the idea of launching a business that could provide economic benefits to women in India and everywhere started to take shape.

In 2019, something amazing happened. Through my networks in India, I found out about innovative social enterprises that upskill women, providing them jobs that pay fair wages, and using recycled yarn made from landfill waste to handweave beautiful textiles. Now, this hit the nail on the head! Following a few discussions with women leaders from these enterprises, I knew I was on the track to commence something big, something powerful to change lives for the better. Since the onset of COVID in 2020, despite numerous lockdowns in Australia and India, we have remained in contact. What prompted me to act? Questions from my then 4-year-old daughter "Can we help?" This gave me enough push to commence planning for sample production and push through despite lockdowns and supply chain crisis.

I had to fight through fears, apprehensions, and negative self-talk plenty of times. I was focusing on my fulfilling and meaningful life, using it as an opportunity to slow down, at times saying to myself that I do not need to rush. Truth be told, it was me stalling because of my fear of failure and ignoring my inner voice that kept guiding me to my soul's purpose.

June 2021 was one of the darkest months in my life. India was grappling with COVID with millions in hospital and countless deaths ravaging almost every family in India. I lost my amazing uncle; a visionary, a leader, a pioneer, a champion of gender equality and community hero. With COVID restrictions and shut borders, I was one of the millions who could not be with their families or say proper goodbye to loved ones. I am incredibly close to my family members and my uncle was like a father figure to me. Losing him hit me hard. My heart was broken – yet I had to find the strength to keep moving forward for the sake of my child, my family and myself.

Melbourne had a 5 km movement restriction. I had to do home schooling, work from home, manage household duties, be supportive of my family, friends, and community while I had grief bubbling deep inside me. But I knew my beloved uncle and my grandmothers would have wanted me to live my truth. During this dark times, I found the courage to accept myself, love myself, unlearn things that were no longer serving me and launch my purpose driven company Punar.

It has taken significant resilience, discipline, and commitment to my vision. With Punar, I have taken a big chance. I have done things I wouldn't have done before. I have sent our beautiful gifts to two South Asian trailblazers, inspiring women founders in USA - no, I didn't hire any PR agency or get introduced by any networks.

The result: these two extraordinary women are using our products; we have received wonderful feedback & Punar on an incredible trajectory. Since launching, Punar has turned 135 kg landfill waste into 925 gifts, paid fair wages to 6 women artisans who have handwoven 420 meters zero emission fabric and received She-Com Editor's Choice Award for eco-friendly and sustainable product category.

I have always found that the harder & smarter I work, I end up in the right place at the right time with the right people. I decided to move past doubts, fear, imposter syndrome and take that risk. My point is if we can get out of our own way, we can create great impact & build a better future.

**What's next?**

I want my daughter and all the children to grow up in a better world than the one we currently live in. Although it's a lofty objective, it serves as my daily motivation. I want a society where gender equality is a given, not an ongoing issue that be fought by generational women.

The future is a blank canvas, and I am prepared with my paintbrush. There will be a mix of personal and professional goals, enriched life with family and friends, anticipation of great things to come and conscious evolution to be a better version of myself. There will be challenges, of course, but if I have learnt anything, it is that often the most challenging times of our lives lead to transformation and re-birth.

As I share my story with you all, I am reflecting on the power of authenticity and purpose. Being our authentic self will pave the way for creating our own dream life. Living our purpose means accepting ourselves just the way we are. I can't help but reiterate that you are the creator of your life, one that is inspiring and empowering, one that leaves the world a little bit better than when you found it. It is your life, your purpose at your own pace.

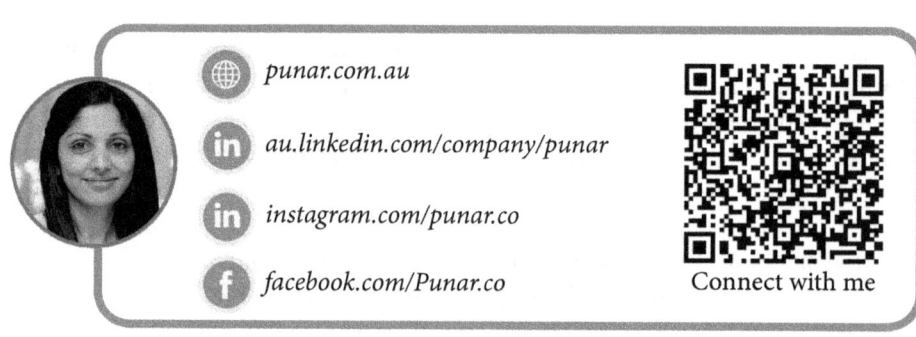

*punar.com.au*

*au.linkedin.com/company/punar*

*instagram.com/punar.co*

*facebook.com/Punar.co*

Connect with me

Chapter 12

# The F-Word. And It's Not What You Think; It's How

**Heidi Stenschke**
*IGlobal Keynote Speaker, Coach, EMDR Clinician,
Hypnotherapist, Yoga Teacher, Master Practitioner and
Trainer of Neuro-Linguistic Programming (NLP), Founder
of Hypnoga®*

## About The Author: Heidi Stenschke

Heidi Stenschke helps people achieve success by teaching them how to be flexible in body and mind, using simple and effective strategies and techniques.

Born at the foothills of the Blue Mountains in NSW, Australia, Heidi is the founder of Hypnoga®, a company coined as 'the latest and greatest fitness and wellness movement' by Forbes Magazine, Morocco. Having featured in multiple international publications, including Digital Online and in numerous local articles, she is a speaker, a hypnotherapist, a yoga teacher, and Master Practitioner and trainer of Neuro Linguistic Programming (NLP).

Heidi's story thus far is one of rags to riches in both mindset and material wealth. Her education spans the two extremes of being expelled at the age of 14 to becoming a Harvard graduate at 36.

From humble beginnings as a machine operator in a food factory, rising to an international advocate for workers in manufacturing, she also became a lead negotiator for state-based and national enterprise agreements. Heidi has also served as a facilitator for industry committees and women's committees and as a director of advisory boards on industry standards.

Both witty and charming, Heidi uses examples from her lived experience peppered with humour to lead and inspire others to challenge the status quo and pursue their dreams.

• • • • •

This F-word can create a bit of a frenzy. Why? Because this particular F-word is code for change. And let's be honest: people don't always like change.

We want it, we need it, we crave it. Yet, we meet it with resistance. Why? It is the same reason we cling to our limitations and our downfalls. Think of the old adage, "Better the devil you know." Most people fight to keep things as they are because it's comfortable, and comfort can seem easy in contrast with the thought of the unknown. The problem with this is that growth and progress require change.

Further, that which we resist is often the doorway to our dreams and desires. To unlock the door, we must be willing to adapt and adopt a new way of thinking. We must be prepared to adjust and align to a new way of being. And if we can befriend this F-word, we can shift from a state of 'stuck' to a state of flow.

There are two F-words to choose from, yet only one can easily unlock the door before you. The first word is inappropriate; the second is **Flexibility.**

To be specific, to move forward in life, we must evolve. We must grow. And any growth that supports human evolution requires:

1. Flexibility of Beliefs
2. Flexibility of Body and Behaviour
3. Flexibility of Language
4. Flexibility of Mind and Thinking

The Law of Requisite Variety states that the system or person with the most flexibility of behaviour will control the system. This law is a principle of NLP and the first law of Cybernetics. Allow me to explain.

As a trainer of Neuro-Linguistic Programming (NLP), a trainer of Hypnotherapy, and an EMDR clinician working to resolve post-traumatic stress disorder (PTSD) and other forms of mental illness, it's fair to say that I know quite a bit about the process humans apply when it comes to thinking. As a yoga teacher, I also have a deep and practical understanding of the movement of the body.

Further, using Hypnoga®, I have helped many of my students shift from a state of 'stuck' both mentally and emotionally, to a state of flow in their body and mind, all through a shift in beliefs.

The ability to be flexible in our beliefs, our body, and our mind may be the single most critical skillset we can learn. This is because when we know how to flex within all these areas, we can adapt to situations and circumstances quickly and readily. We can arrive at any scene armed with knowledge and wisdom, and still show up present, curious, and open to the unknown.

I have discovered that learning NLP opens doors that would have otherwise remained locked. These life-changing skills offer a new way of thinking that just makes sense. When you learn NLP, you learn a level of flexibility that leads to:

- Understanding the intricacies of effective communication,
- Understanding the benefits of intentional physiology, and
- Understanding why people behave the way they do.

You see, we define Neuro-Linguistic Programming (NLP) in many ways. It is a study of excellence and a model of how individuals structure their experience. NLP is also an effective series of techniques that enable my students to create radical change within themselves and the clients they serve. I teach them to do this in terms of context rather than content.

Ultimately, I teach people how to think, not what to think. I teach my students how to critically analyse any situation across any context, be it business, therapy, or education, as well as in personal and professional relationships. The key component in all that we do is the ability to be flexible in beliefs, thinking, language, and behaviour.

Dr. Weitzenhoffer, a respected expert in the field of hypnosis who devoted almost his entire professional life to its study said, "In hypnosis, your client will not actualise what the hypnotherapist does not believe." This belief, also applied in NLP, helps to frame our thinking to ensure that we approach our work with an open mind.

To further support this, in our school of NLP training, we believe that everyone is magnificent and has unlimited potential. We believe that as long as specific criteria are met, we can actualise anything we put our minds to! Adopting these beliefs helps us to support and guide our clients in achieving their goals harmoniously and congruently.

Again, The Law of Requisite Variety states that the system or person with the most flexibility of behaviour will control the system. Let me give you a few examples.

## 1. Flexibility of Beliefs

When I told a friend I was writing a chapter on flexibility, and I explained that it included the need to be flexible in our beliefs, she responded in shock. She looked at me in horror, wondering if I was attacking her religion, which was not my intention at all. What I am doing is asking you to consider your own beliefs, and when you do, ask yourself: are they even yours?

For example, take the stern parents who refrained from expressing emotions. These parents raised their children to believe expressing emotions was a sign of weakness. No tenderness in a spoken word; no intimacy or physical touch. There were no hugs on birthdays. No reassuring gestures after a knee graze from a skateboard accident. No warm embrace after a teenage heartbreak. Nothing. Only instructions like, "Pick yourself up, dust yourself off, and move on." Fast forward 25 years to when those children are now parents themselves, and the family tradition continues. "We don't do that touchy-feely stuff in this family."

Here's another example; it's Christmas morning, and the daughter observes her mother cutting both ends off the roast before placing it in the oven. "Mum, why do you do that?" Mum casually replies, "Well, your grandma always did this. And so, I do, too. It's tradition." "Why did Grandma do it?" the daughter asked. "I'm not sure," Mum answered. "Why don't you ask her when she arrives for Christmas lunch?" Grandma comes, and the daughter asks her the same question. "Grandma, every year, Mum cuts off the ends of the roast before placing it in the oven. She learned this from you. Why did you do that?" Grandma chuckled. "Because our oven was too small; it wouldn't fit in if I didn't!"

Most of our beliefs are instilled in us as children. It is known in many fields that until the age of seven, children are like sponges. We accept almost everything uncritically especially the beliefs of our parents or caregivers. As good as their intentions may be, these bestowed beliefs are rarely reviewed to consider if we actually agree with them. Yet, we are often quick to defend them if challenged.

I am not saying that we should discard all beliefs or that all beliefs are not our own. I am saying that it would serve us to take stock of our beliefs, review them, and then make a conscious decision as to whether we want to keep them or not. Particularly as beliefs are the root cause of habits and behaviours.

Consider the following statement:

All behaviour stems from a belief. To change a behaviour, we must change the belief.

Let's use the analogy of a fruit tree. A seed (belief) is planted (accepted) in the soil (mind). The environment (body) nourishes the seed (belief) and it grows. It continues to grow and continues to produce the fruit (behaviour). Therefore, plant a different seed, produce a different fruit. or Change the belief, produce a new behaviour.

Now consider the previous example of the Christmas roast.

Mum's behaviour of cutting the ends off the roast originated from the belief that it was tradition. She blindly accepted this belief and happily upheld the 'tradition'. When the daughter questioned her mum's behaviour, she was able to identify its origin as well as the belief that caused it. In doing so, she was empowered to choose to continue with the 'tradition', or not.

In short, change the belief, change the behaviour.

## 2. Flexibility of Language

It serves us to consider the components of communication. As is taught at the NLP Practitioner Level, communication consists of:

- 7% words
- 38% voice/tonality
- 55% physiology/body language

This means 93% of all communication is non-verbal. Let's pause here for a moment. Only 7% of communication is the words we use! This rings true in the phrase 'actions speak louder than words' and 'it's not what you say, it's how you say it'.

It is helpful to understand the relationship between communication and the five senses (sight/visual, hearing/auditory, feeling/kinaesthetic, taste/gustatory, smell/olfactory).

In NLP, the five senses are referred to as Representational Systems (RS), and we recognise that each of us favours one over the other. We also add in Auditory Digital; this is our inner dialogue, or self-talk and the words we use to label our experiences.

Each RS can be further broken down into sub-categories called 'predicates'. Predicates are simply specific words that are used relative to each RS for example, for the representational system of 'Sight', we could use predicates such as 'visualise, imagine or look'. For the representational system of 'Sound', we could use predicates such as 'hear, loud or resonate'. To further illustrate, consider a salesperson making an offer to a customer to purchase an item:

- A person who favours the visual RS might respond, "I will look into it," or "Let me see."
- A person who favours the auditory RS might respond, "It sounds ok," or "It doesn't resonate for me."
- A person who favours the kinaesthetic RS might respond, "Let me get a feel for it," or "I just can't put my finger on it."

These are all subtly different responses showing predicates from various representational systems. What does this have to do with the flexibility of language?

The answer is simple. People naturally speak using predicates from their preferred representational system, and when you are aware of it, you get valuable information. Understanding this enables you to not only learn people's preferences by paying attention to the language they use, but you can also communicate with a person using their preferred choice of words. This increases your chances of your message getting through to your audience.

After all, people don't hear what you say, they hear their interpretation of what you say. Given words are only 7% of communication, precision of appropriate language can maximise the effectiveness of this component of communication. It's worth learning.

**Key Takeaway:** flexibility in language increases your ability to connect with, and influence others.

### 3. Flexibility of Body and Behaviour

Let's start with the obvious. Increasing flexibility in the physical body is not about being a contortionist. While we may not aspire to wrap our legs around our necks, movement beyond rigid regimes allows us to increase our range of motion. It can also result in lengthening and strengthening of the body to maintain primary, functional movement and avoid preventable aches and niggles.

As body language is the greatest component of communication, it is critical that you are aware of your own physiology. Secondly, it helps to have a repertoire of movements and gestures appropriate to your intended message and desired outcome.

Further, given communication is 55% physiology, even if you master the art of language, the message our physiology sends will trump the spoken word. Our physiology will either enhance our message or, if it's incongruent with what we say, may create mistrust with our audience. Even if your audience can't articulate why they don't trust you, they will undoubtedly feel the disconnect between what they hear, what they see, and what they feel. Remember: "Actions speak louder than words."

In NLP, we teach Sensory Acuity, a skill on observing and interpreting physiology.

This is not about mind-reading; this is about noticing things such as posture, facial expressions and even the pace of a person's breathing. This is all data. It is information that provides insight and suggestions as to how your audience is feeling about you, and what you have to say. This data allows you to adjust and align so that you can better connect and serve your client.

**Key Takeaway:** If it is your job to communicate effectively and influence others, flexibility in physiology is essential.

### 4. Flexibility in Mind and Thinking

In my training, NLP is taught in 2 levels. Level 1 is for the Practitioner, and level 2 is for the Master Practitioner. On the first day of level 1, we unpack, in detail, what we call the Presuppositions of NLP, or 'Convenient Assumptions'. We invite our students to adopt these convenient assumptions as they help to frame our mindset to achieve success in the work that we do.

There are 14 Convenient Assumptions in NLP. To help illustrate flexibility in thinking, I am going to introduce you to four of them using my own personal examples.

**Convenient Assumption #1: Calibrate on Behaviour: The most important information about a person is that person's behaviour.**

The shop assistant scanned my groceries aggressively; he was not happy! It was a local family-owned store whose unique selling point was high-quality customer service. Accordingly, customers were usually met with high energy and a warm welcome. While his words were, "Hi, how are you?" his voice was monotone, and his body language screamed, "I can't be bothered; I hate my job and don't want to be here."

Demanding he improve his behaviour based on store policy would likely get my eggs broken. But I was beginning to feel frustrated with his frustration! I took a breath. And I paused.

Sure, I could have kept quiet, waited for my groceries to be packed, and then left with my newly acquired frustration. But I chose not to.

Instead, I acknowledged his frustrations and began building rapport as I enquired about his day and his well-being. I noticed his physiology shift. His shoulders dropped, and his eyes softened as he looked at me, properly, for the first time. He apologized for being rude. We exchanged smiles as I listened to him talk about his partner's shenanigans as he calmly packed my groceries.

It turned out that his behaviour was out of character, and he was 'having a moment.' Now, when I go shopping, he greets me with a smile and sometimes even opens his register especially for me.

**Key Takeaway:** My ability to see past his words and calibrate on his behaviour enabled me to connect with him and improve our state and the overall experience.

**Convenient Assumption #2: People are not their behaviours.**

(Accept the person; change the behaviour.)

Helen was rude and arrogant, and she spoke over others during the meeting. Her body was leaned forward, and she used a lot of finger-pointing to express her view. Her voice was loud, her gaze direct, and her eyebrows furrowed. The team was in shock and barely said a word.

It was Helen's first week on the job. Her resume was glowing with all the required attributes, and she performed very well in the interview. As much as the company required her skillset, we needed Helen to gel with the team.

I befriended Helen, and we quickly established rapport. Helen confided in me that she was new to town and had come from a place where she was not permitted to speak, let alone contribute. She previously did her work remotely and the office environment was new to her. She'd wanted to fit in, and also wanted to be respected. Knowing this, the intense behaviour displayed in that meeting made sense.

I gave Helen tactful feedback regarding her behaviour and she welcomed my suggestions. She approached the next meeting differently, and the team quickly warmed to Helen. She was kind, smart and very funny and turned out to be an excellent fit for our team.

**Key Takeaway:** Helen's behaviour at the first meeting deterred the others from wanting to work with her. Understanding that people are not their behaviours allowed me to see past the behaviour and connect with Helen as a person.

**Convenient Assumptions #3: Resistance in a client is a sign of a lack of rapport.**

(There are no resistant clients, only inflexible communicators. Effective communicators accept and utilize all communication presented to them.)

I enjoyed door-to-door sales, selling back-to-base security monitoring for residential properties, and one day, we had an incredible 50% discount if customers would sign up on the spot. Additionally, the team who made the most sales would receive a bonus cash prize. There were two teams from two states, and I was not on my home ground.

As I approached one home, a couple in their 60s had just pulled into their driveway from grocery shopping. "Good morning," I said cheerfully. I helped carry their groceries, we exchanged niceties, and then I explained the details of the fantastic offer.

They were very interested. They told me they had been thinking about a security system, and suddenly I showed up! As keen as they were, they said, "Not now," and kindly but firmly asked me to return the next day. I respected their request and sadly walked on to the next house. I knew I wouldn't get the bonus if I didn't close that day.

So, I walked back and stated my case. I pivoted from the facts of the excellent deal, and I explained my predicament. While they appreciated the great offer, they valued my sincerity more. They understood I would not receive the credit if I didn't close that day and made me a cup of tea while we signed the contract.

**Key Takeaway:** The couple valued the benefits of the offer, yet they were not willing to sign based on the facts alone. Using my Sensory Acuity (a technique taught in the 7-day NLP Practitioner Training), I detected their positive response to my friendliness and mannerisms. I shifted my focus from the facts and appealed to their emotions to create a win-win situation and seal the deal.

**Convenient Assumption #4: The Law of Requisite Variety states that the system or person with the most flexibility of behaviour will control the system.**

This Convenient Assumption has appeared several times in this chapter, and it is not an accident. The ability to be flexible in our behaviour stems from first being flexible in our beliefs and our thinking.

I have reiterated this point again and again because it is my heartfelt desire to encourage you to review your beliefs. Not because I gain from it, but because when we do review our beliefs, we can differentiate between beliefs that belong to us and beliefs that are bestowed. We begin the shift towards a life that aligns with our true beliefs; the ones that guide us with a gut feeling or an inner knowing. Let's call this our truth.

When our beliefs are congruent with our truth, a change in mindset occurs. Our behaviours adjust and our language shifts. We begin to get a grasp on who we really are, by nature. When we are confident with living as nature intended, we are better able to witness the true nature of others. We can see beyond their bestowed beliefs, and this enables us to be proactive, instead of reactive in our response. In confronting or difficult times, we learn to accept the person and change the behaviour.

We are many things in our lives: a parent, a child, a spouse, a colleague, a boss, a worker. As an individual connected to this network called existence, this F-word, friends, is synonymous with change. When we accept that change is inevitable, we can choose to act to influence it according to our truth. This is true power. And this power is what we get when we become flexible in our beliefs, in our thinking, in our language and in our behaviour.

Book Heidi to speak at your next event.

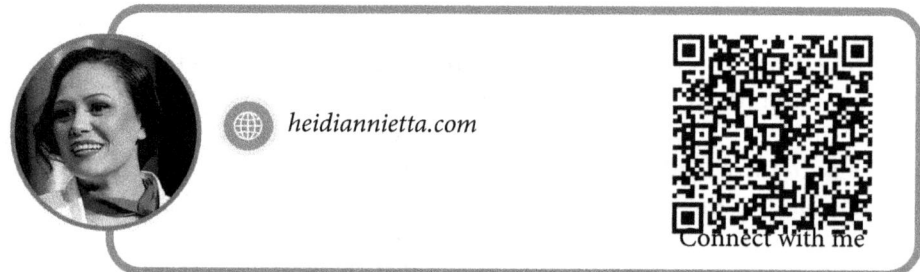

heidiannietta.com

Connect with me

www.ingramcontent.com/pod-product-compliance
Lightning Source LLC
Chambersburg PA
CBHW050636160426
43194CB00010B/1699